HOW TO BUILD A
FASHION ICON

HOW TO BUILD A
FASHION ICON

NOTES ON
CONFIDENCE

FROM THE
WORLD'S ONLY
IMAGE ARCHITECT

LAW ROACH

ABRAMS IMAGE, NEW YORK

Editor: Soyolmaa Lkhagvadorj
Designer: Diane Shaw
Managing Editor: Lisa Silverman
Production Manager: Sarah Masterson Hally

Library of Congress Control Number: 2024935813

ISBN: 978-1-4197-6821-7
eISBN: 979-8-88707-033-9

ABRAMS The Art of Books
195 Broadway, New York, NY 10007
abramsbooks.com

CONTENTS

FOREWORD BY JEREMY SCOTT   IX

Introduction: The Image Architect   1

Chapter 1: Let the Transformation Begin   8

Chapter 2: Assessing Your Foundations   24

Chapter 3: Crafting Your Style Story   46

Chapter 4: Don't Be Afraid to Be Unique   65

Chapter 5: Always Stay Inspired   87

Chapter 6: Love Yourself   103

Chapter 7: Manifest and Reflect   123

Chapter 8: The Renaissance Era   142

Conclusion   159

ACKNOWLEDGMENTS   161

ABOUT THE AUTHOR   163

DEDICATION

There are so many people who made it possible for me to write this book, but before we get started, there's one important person I'd like to dedicate this work to. She is my little sister, my muse, my close collaborator, and my biggest advocate: Zendaya Coleman.

I have had many clients in this industry—so many stunning women (and even men), some of whom I write about in this book—but I have only had one fashion sibling. Zendaya, you and I came into this industry together. As a teenager you trusted me and listened to me even when I didn't know it was my responsibility as a stylist to bring safety pins to a fitting (as you like to remind me). You believed in yourself and allowed me to mold you into the fashion icon I always knew you could be. Even before you could see the vision, you trusted in me, and that trust allowed me to do this work at the level I've reached.

You've been loyal and stood beside me through this long and winding journey, bringing me into rooms I could only dream of being in. And you speak my name, telling the world how I inspired you and taught you about confidence and speaking up for yourself. We have become the perfect collaborators, together helping to figure not only the big picture but the small details.

It's rare that someone like me receives such support from someone they are working for. Bringing your stylist onto the Met Gala red carpet to act out the Cinderella fairy tale we have lived through (*wink*) is something no one else would do. But no one else has the relationship we have.

Without you this book would not have been possible, so it's important to me to say thank you. Thank you for being the vessel through which the world got a chance to see my ability. And hopefully you don't mind if I let the world into a few of our secrets in the next few pages.

FOREWORD BY
JEREMY SCOTT

I have had the pleasure of collaborating with many incredible and talented people throughout my career. But the one who stands out as undeniably unique is Law Roach. Law can't simply be categorized as a "stylist"—he transcends the term. He is a tastemaker, a style activist, and . . . an "image architect," a term cleverly coined by Law and one that he lives up to in every sense!

Law has created some of the most memorable and dramatic editorial and red-carpet moments of recent times. I have worked with him on numerous occasions and witnessed his vivid imagination and compelling vision firsthand. Law does not just draw upon fashion as inspiration. He brilliantly draws from film, art, history, and architecture to create new pop culture moments himself!

Law has never shied away from his humble beginnings in the South Side of Chicago. Instead, he's infused the cultural richness of his street style into the work he presents today. Law's story and trajectory are, in every sense, the epitome of the American Dream. His deep connection to equality and diversity propels him to use his platform to amplify social causes, to give back, and to uplift others.

In this book, Law uses his humor, wit, creativity, and honesty to show how inclusivity can change the narrative of fashion. Everyone has something unique that makes them special. This book is a beautiful reminder to celebrate those values in every way.

THE
IMAGE ARCHITECT

E veryone who lives and breathes fashion knows the importance of the Council of Fashion Designers of America's Fashion Awards. On November 10, 2021, the Pool and the Grill restaurant in Midtown Manhattan's Seagram Building was packed for them. Emily Blunt, Ciara, Drew Barrymore, Aubrey Plaza, Karlie Kloss, Cara Delevingne, and J Balvin were all there, sitting around crowded tables. Onstage was the supermodel Iman, looking stunning in a draped black gown. Having been crowned a Fashion Icon in 2010 by the Council of Fashion Designers of America (CFDA), Iman had returned to pass the baton.

"Zendaya is one of the youngest icons to inspire and excite the world with her great sense of style," she said into the mic. "And she's certainly one of the most fearless. Her instincts and confidence on the red carpet have redefined glamour for an entire new generation of fashion lovers . . . Zendaya reminds us that true icons must always be brave, and they will be forever ageless."

It was a *moment*. I felt tears in my eyes as I watched Zendaya go up onstage. She was wearing an all-red custom look from Vera Wang that night. We had opted for a column skirt with a peplum, bandeau top, and cropped jacket. It probably wasn't what people expected from her (or Vera), but we'd gone with it anyway.

As Zendaya accepted her Fashion Icon Award, I couldn't help but wonder how we got there. I wasn't onstage with her in person, but I had been her only stylist her entire career. Even in her acceptance speech she called me her co-director in fashion.

"My fashion soulmate, historian, and constant inspiration," she said. "Thank you for pushing me to see all of myself and teaching me how to do so fearlessly." Zendaya was the youngest person ever named Fashion Icon by the CFDA, joining global stars like Lady Gaga, Beyoncé, and Pharrell. And she was also probably the only one to consistently work with one stylist in her entire career. But what had brought us to the "Oscars of fashion"? How did we make a fashion icon? And how could someone else repeat it?

When I sit back and think about it, the answer is clear: it takes being *you*. To be a fashion icon is about the confidence you radiate when you walk into a room. That is the core belief that I've based my whole career on. And here, in the pages of this book, that's what I'm going to help you cultivate.

I've been blessed to work with some of the most influential and powerful celebrities of our time—people who command attention every time they step outside. But what makes these people undeniable fashion icons is not the clothes in which they're photographed. No. What makes Zendaya *Zendaya* and Céline *Céline* is their ferocity. Their fearlessness. Their unabashed confidence in themselves. Their clothes are an extension of who they are—a vehicle through which they can channel their power, vision, and values. Ultimately, I've built a career on helping clients find *themselves*.

My start in styling was unusual. I never had the opportunity to be an assistant or an intern. I never studied under any of the greats, though many have been kind and supportive over the years. I never learned someone else's approach and methodology. I just always knew that I could do it. I believed in (and bet on) myself at all costs.

Because I didn't know how anyone else did it, my styling process mirrors that of constructing a building. I'm not simply putting clothes on a body; I'm laying foundations, designing a story, sourcing materials, and lifting someone up. That process requires deep research; a thorough understanding of the client's vision; a detailed design to build from; the right team of contractors to bring it to life (hair, makeup, design); and an ability to inspire people to trust in themselves, their work, and their vision. It's a skill set I've honed over many years, and it's proven invaluable to me.

That's why I coined the term "Image Architect." I could never be just a "stylist"—I'm always doing things my own way, with my own spin. When I came up with it, everyone was a multi-hyphenate. You would look at someone's Instagram bio, and it would say they were a stylist-photographer-creative director. I wanted to stand out. To me, an Image Architect delivers a moment—the boldness and drama of a look complemented by a woman (or anyone, to be honest) who knows their worth. I'm not the first person in fashion to see the similarities between industries. Coco Chanel once said, "Fashion is architecture," and multiple fashion designers like Virgil Abloh, Pierre Balmain, Tom Ford, and Thierry Mugler all studied architecture before going into design. But I was the first to call myself by this title.

> I could never be just a "stylist"— I'm always doing things my own way, with my own spin.

I'm the world's only Image Architect, in fact. I hold the trademark. And now I'm ready to share my secrets with you.

I've never been interested in helping just a select, rarefied few. I truly believe that everyone deserves to feel confident within themselves. Everyone deserves to be an icon in whatever they choose to wear and all they choose to do. It is my hope that this book—through its tips, tricks, and recipes—will teach you how to do exactly that. Through our work together, you'll take the steps to discover and fully embrace your authentic self. The best part is, we don't need much: Everything you need to become the best, most confident version of yourself is already inside of you.

At the heart of everything I've ever done is my desire to amplify that confidence in people. As a kid, growing up in a rough neighborhood in Chicago, I stood my ground against anyone who wanted to change who I was and remained unapologetically myself. Later, as an up-and-coming stylist, that same belief allowed me to push myself, to rely on my instincts and intuition when it seemed like everyone around me had connections and experience. I might not have the pedigree, the elite education, or the long-held connections, but I know who I am and what I bring to the table. That has opened doors for me and will do the same for you.

In *How to Build a Fashion Icon*, I'm sharing my experiences and the lessons learned from working with icons like Zendaya, Ariana Grande, and Céline Dion. These women, among many others, have taught me so much over the last decade. But most of all, I'll tell you how *you* can become a Fashion Icon in your own life.

While we may not all have access to the same resources or clothes, there are simple things that everyone can do to live their most authentic, iconic, and fashionable lives. With this book, I offer readers the ultimate guide to channeling their inner grace and confidence to learn how to love themselves and become the person they were always meant to be.

Before we even get started, I'm going to let you in on the biggest secret in fashion. Actually, no. This is the biggest secret in *life*, one that I've known the power of since I was a kid. The secret to success, to happiness, to fulfillment, and to continually challenging yourself to do and be more is confidence.

The secret to being a fashion icon is not a Vera Wang gown or a custom Valentino. You don't have to be Zendaya on the cover of *Vogue* or Anya Taylor-Joy accepting a Golden Globe. It's confidence. Ultimately, fashion isn't just about putting on a pretty dress; it's about creating a moment, one that is rooted in self-assurance.

How to Build a Fashion Icon is here to give you the tools you need to find, sharpen, and grow that confidence. It is the beginning of your bold, beautiful new life. When you're confident, the clothes you put on are simply an outward expression of what is within. They highlight and accentuate, but they don't define who you are. Only you can do that.

When we are done here, you'll be able to look at yourself in the mirror at the end of each day and truly believe it when you say, "You did what needed to be done."

Let's get started.

"Fashion you can buy, but style you possess. The key to style is learning who you are, which takes years. There's no how-to road map to style. It's about self-expression, and above all, attitude."

—IRIS APFEL, FROM THE 2014 DOCUMENTARY *IRIS*

01.

LET THE TRANSFORMATION BEGIN

On March 14, 2023, I announced my retirement. It was the morning after the Oscars, one of the biggest nights in Hollywood and in celebrity styling. I had styled five of the most gorgeous women in the world for the *Vanity Fair* Oscar Party, and the looks I created were front and center in the press, lauded as the best of the night. It was an evening that should have been one of my greatest career achievements. But it just wasn't.

On that particular morning, I knew I couldn't go on the way I had been. For me, styling has always been an exercise in creativity. It's been instinctual, actually. I'll find myself inspired by something and then I'll know in my gut what the right decisions are. But more and more, I was being hounded to perform this art on demand. The need for everything to happen immediately was wearing on me and had begun to cause a tremendous amount of anxiety that was impacting my health. A change was needed, and I knew I had to make my announcement before I lost my nerve. I posted the word "Retired" in red, across a white background, on Instagram.

"If this business was just about the clothes I would do it for the rest of my life but unfortunately, it's not!" I wrote in the caption, nervous, anxious, and deeply emotional. "The politics, the lies and false narratives finally got me!" The fact is, I was in tears when I posted the news. But I also felt certain. I knew I was making the right choice. After a decade of putting everything and everyone before myself, I knew it was time to make this change.

I was at the top of my game—I had been named the most powerful stylist in Hollywood, the CFDA had given me their first-ever Stylist Award, and my clients were widely regarded as the best dressed on red carpets. On the Internet, fans of celebrities would tag me in comment sections to ask if I would work with their favorites. But emotionally and spiritually, I was running on empty. My plan was uncertain, but I knew I needed to step back from celebrity styling and the way that I had been of service to other people for so long.

Fashion will forever be in my blood, and I knew that I would continue my work in other areas within the industry. But at that moment, I needed something new, which meant getting away from celebrity styling. I needed to transform my life in a way that would fill up my cup, provide new challenges and opportunities, and remove some of the weight of other people's expectations.

It's difficult to leave a successful career, one that seemed from the outside to be so glamorous and fulfilling. I knew there were many who wouldn't understand. For days, I read the comments on social media, and I was really moved by the support and love I was shown. To walk away from this career that I built while I was very much at the top of my game required so much strength and every ounce of confidence I had. I needed to put myself first. And the reason I could do that was because I was confident my skills would make everything work out in the end. No matter what.

THE KEY IS CONFIDENCE

There's something about seeing someone else achieve an accolade, receive an award, or break new ground that often feels distant or inaccessible to us. There's a *that could never be me* mentality. *There must be some reason, some unseen force, some connection or advantage that I don't have that's standing in my way.* Years ago, I used to sometimes think that.

Let me put a stop to that thought right here and now: It most certainly can be you. You can do and be and achieve anything you want to. Allow me to be the example of an unlikely Cinderella story, of someone who grew up with the cards stacked against them but did it anyway.

Here's how I did it: unwavering, deep-seated, cellularly activated confidence.

Confidence is the belief in oneself and in one's abilities. It comes from understanding that self-worth isn't measured by achievements, failures, or the opinions of others. Confidence is not necessarily determined by the people around you—don't wait for people to validate you. Building self-confidence can be a multistep process, but don't let it discourage you.

When you see a client of mine on the red carpet or in a magazine, what you're seeing is the final product of weeks and often months of work. And while I am talking about the process of pulling looks, going through fittings, and deciding on the hair and makeup, the inner work is often the most essential. There is a reason that people fell in love with clips of Megan Thee Stallion in a vintage 1997 Paco Rabanne two-piece look at *The Hollywood Reporter* and Jimmy Choo's Power Stylists dinner. Yes, the seventies-inspired bikini top and low-rise, wide-leg pants all in gold were perfect, but what people were really applauding was that they could sense she felt like she was "that girl." *Billboard* magazine called her a "golden goddess," *Glamour* called her "a vision," and we all wanted to be her. It was much the same way at the 2018 Academy Awards when I put Tom Holland in a custom Hermès double-breasted tuxedo that got him named one of the best dressed by British *GQ* and *Esquire*. That night, he transformed into an adult in the eyes of many. And sure, a perfectly tailored, smart suit can help shape that idea, but the clothes were just a reflection of what was already inside.

Early in my career, Zendaya and I were at New York Fashion Week. This was 2014, so

Confidence is not necessarily determined by the people around you—don't wait for people to validate you.

she was not the global megastar and fashion icon you know her as today. Yes, I knew it (and told her at every opportunity), but the world wasn't aware just yet. This particular day I convinced her to go to Lincoln Center, where the shows were then held. We didn't have an invitation for a specific show, but I wanted the photographers and the world to see that this was the most beautiful girl in the world. They needed to see what I saw. So I pulled out a yellow and blue Miuniku coat that I had packed for her with some destroyed Rag & Bone jeans and a white shirt from Acne, and she did her own hair and makeup. Off we went.

When we arrived and Z began walking on the snow-packed side-walk, a few photographers took notice. Some asked a few questions—most didn't even know her name. We heard the shutter of a few cameras. I whispered in her ear: "They aren't photographing you because you're a celebrity, they are photographing you because you're beautiful." I wasn't lying to her, and I never would—it was the truth, and it was important she knew it! Four photographers became six; six became ten. I watched her stand up a little taller, and the elegance we both knew she possessed became a touch more prominent. The photographers became a mob that returned day after day for the rest of that week, photographing anything and everything she wore. She ended up being covered by *WWD* and *The Fashion Police*, but that small moment was the launch of a new street-style darling with noth-ing more than some denim, a color-blocked coat, and confidence.

Anyone can afford that.

START BUILDING YOUR CONFIDENCE

People will tell you that self-confidence is a sort of innate or natural thing, but that's not always true. Like almost anything else in life, it is a skill that you can hone with practice. Building confidence is a gradual process that involves self-awareness, practice, and self-acceptance. It might not cost you much money, but it will take time. Ultimately, though, it's an investment in yourself: Confidence can help you excel in all you pursue professionally and personally, helping you to perform better at work, making you unafraid of stepping into leadership positions, and emboldening you with courage to take on new opportunities.

The road to confidence is a long one, so be patient with yourself. If you're new to the journey, don't be afraid. Here are some steps to start building your confidence, whether you've picked up this book to learn the basics or need a quick reminder today.

HOW YOU TALK TO YOURSELF MATTERS

It's true. How you speak to yourself affects not only your daily mood, but it can transform the way you see yourself. Start by monitoring your inner dialogue throughout the day. Replace any self-criticism and negative self-talk with positive affirmations. Replace self-doubt with self-compassion and remind yourself of your strengths and accomplishments. Instead of saying, "I can't do this," say, "I will do my best, and I can learn from any mistakes." Remember, don't compare yourself to anyone: What's for you is for you and there is only one of you. Live and excel in that fact.

ACKNOWLEDGE YOUR STRENGTHS

If your first instinct is to say, "But Law, what if I don't have strengths to acknowledge?" I would say you need to push past that and dig a little deeper. Everyone has strengths—no matter how big or small—that are unique to you. Make a list of your strengths, skills, and past achievements starting with "I am really great at . . ." or "No one can do . . . the way I can." Reminding yourself of your past can give you more stability moving into your future. Then make one of these positive affirmations or strengths into the screensaver on your phone. We all look at our phones a million times a day to unlock it. You'll read it so many times, it will become ingrained. Try it for a day, a week, or six months and then change it. It's like having your very own Law Roach whispering in your ear.

VOCALIZE YOUR STRENGTHS

Now, say out loud what you want to believe. Share your wins and accomplishments vocally with others. It may feel uncomfortable at first to walk into a party and say, "Damn I look good today," or to sit at your family dinner and start by saying, "I did really good today," but it's important. Start by vocalizing to yourself in the mirror, and then do so with others. People will start to see you as you see yourself. And most importantly, you'll start to believe it even if you don't at first.

LEARN NEW TRICKS AND DEVELOP SKILLS.

Get out of your head and try something new. Push yourself out of your comfort zone by trying a new hobby or skill. You might fall flat on your face, and that's OK. It's all part of the process, because inevitably you will learn something from the experience. When you gradually expose yourself to situations that make you uncomfortable or anxious, you can expand your comfort zone and build confidence in the process.

Here's a great way to build your confidence in introducing yourself and interacting with others while trying something new: Go on social media and go live. Use it as a way to introduce yourself to new people. It doesn't matter if you have two people or two hundred people joining. Introduce yourself and talk about whatever facets of your background, personality, or favorites that you feel like sharing. It can help build character and toughen your skin. If you've never done that, it can be really scary to put yourself out there, but that's the point of it—pushing through discomfort is how you grow. If it becomes too much, give yourself small windows like five minutes. But if you can do it on live, you can do it in a social setting.

If you're worried that going live might be too much too soon, you can just try it in real life: The next time you go to an event or party, introduce yourself to two people by the end of the night. Every time it goes well, you'll get a little boost of extra confidence. And if one goes not so well, hop back on the horse as soon as possible and remind yourself that another opportunity is always waiting.

CELEBRATE SMALL WINS

Don't underestimate the power of celebrating even small achievements. Recognizing your progress can boost your confidence and motivation. Treat yourself! Book a manicure, buy your favorite magazine, or take a friend out for coffee. These rewards can be a great way to celebrate a win without breaking the bank.

You can even take a selfie and post it on social media. Make your caption "I did it" without divulging the details on what exactly, and let the comments roll in with people congratulating you. But let them wonder what you did specifically. If they ask what you did, you don't have to respond—some details aren't for the public. This helps prevent you from putting too much importance on outside validation from others. You don't need others to weigh in on your choices. You're posting for you because you're proud of yourself.

What small win can you celebrate today?

THERE ARE NO FAILURES

Be grateful for perceived failures. If you fail a test in college, be grateful for the opportunity to learn and understand the subject. If you don't get a job you applied for, be grateful that the universe is keeping you from something that wasn't the fit you thought it would be. There is so much confidence that can come from seeing a setback as an opportunity to learn and grow, rather than as a reflection of your abilities.

The bigger thinking here is simple: the universe protects. If something just isn't working no matter how hard you try, it isn't a failure; it is the universe's protection. You're being guided in a different direction.

Remember that building confidence is an ongoing journey. Be patient with yourself and acknowledge that confidence may fluctuate on any given day, week, or month. Progress is not always linear, and setbacks are a normal part of growth. Developing a positive and resilient mindset will allow you to face challenges with self-assurance and continue to grow as an individual.

CONFIDENCE IS A MUSCLE

I believe that clothing is the first line of defense, a coat of armor, in presenting who you are to the world. It can help project your confidence: how you wear clothing is often a reflection of your inner self-perception. But through this book you'll also learn that what you put on can help shape your confidence as well. Walking through this world can be challenging, and if you can identify exactly what jeans or what colors make you feel the most beautiful and pulled together, then you'll be one step closer to holding your head high and exuding confidence.

When a confident woman walks in a room, it does not matter what she's wearing. Truly. It doesn't matter about her race or ethnicity, her hair color, her body type, or her age. There is something innate about confidence that we are all attracted to as human beings. We are often physiologically attracted to that thing without even knowing that's what we're attracted to. Maybe you call it charisma, or vibes, or even swag. Whatever it is, everyone has some way of acknowledging it when they see it firsthand.

The power of clothes is that we get to be whoever we want to be.

If you walk into a room and you're feeling good and you're confident, others are going to notice that and respond to it. Somebody in that room, if not everybody, is going to notice that. This book is to help you find that extra "oomph."

Think of confidence as a muscle. Some people, because of their genetics and experience, might "naturally" be a little more muscular than you are. Maybe they adapt to physical activities a little easier than others or are able to lift heavier weights more quickly. But with the proper training and time, anyone can do it. This book is a collection of workouts for your confidence muscle. Within these pages you can expect to find exercises you can return to time and time again until your confidence becomes second nature and ingrained in who you are. It's the key to unlocking so many doors in your life, including standing out as a fashion icon.

No matter where you find yourself on a daily basis—strutting down the streets of West Hollywood on your way to a business lunch, reshelving books at your local library in the Midwest, or going to your neighborhood bodega—you have the opportunity to be an icon. You can put your best foot forward every single day to look, and more importantly, feel your best.

If you wake up in the morning and you put on your favorite outfit, it sets you up to have a better day. When you feel confident and comfortable in an outfit, it can boost your self-esteem and overall mood. This is the power of style. It's not about how you look in clothes, it's about how you feel in an outfit. The power of clothes is that we get to be whoever we want to be.

Clothes are a beautiful, fun, and playful way to show the world who you are. But the confidence you bring to the table makes all the difference. Icon status is all about you. And remember: *Wear the clothes, don't let the clothes wear you.*

When you find your confidence, you'll begin to let go of the comparison game and no longer worry what others are doing. You'll realize that everyone else has their own identities and messages that they're communicating so there is no point in comparing yourself to them. You will start to celebrate the little details that make you different, rather than striving to fit in with those around you. It is not about wearing clothes that are "in style" or trendy, or being a person others admire for having "good style." You will learn that good style is a myth, and the only thing that truly exists is personal style.

Confidence is a key element in making a fashion statement that truly stands out. I always encourage my clients to embrace their individuality and wear their clothing choices with confidence.

The right outfit can boost someone's confidence and empower them to feel their best. I believe that when you feel good about what you're wearing, it shows in your demeanor and how you present yourself to the world. Confidence is about owning your choices, celebrating your uniqueness, and radiating authenticity.

My tastes and aesthetics have changed over the years, but my philosophy as a stylist has always remained the same. I never impose my style onto clients. Instead, I look at what she, uniquely, brings to the table, and I work with her to discover the story she wants to tell. When I find what makes her feel her most confident—not just a piece of clothing or a silhouette but a feeling, a mood, a specific item that evokes power and boldness—I will lean even more into that vision for her. Style is timeless. This may be controversial, but I don't believe in trends, and I don't believe in dressing for your body type. I believe in wearing what makes you feel like the powerful, capable badass that you are.

Clothes are truly transformative; they are able to shift your reality to the one you dream and fantasize about. But you have to know yourself, because that's ultimately where the confidence comes from.

IT'S NEVER TOO LATE TO START OVER

One of the biggest compliments I've received as a stylist is that none of my clients look the same. If you know the business, you know that many stylists have a signature aesthetic that informs the looks they develop for their clients—in fact, stylists are often hired for that specific aesthetic alone. But for me, it's the inverse. Ariana Grande has never looked like Kerry Washington under my guidance. Kerry Washington has never looked like Zendaya. Zendaya has never looked like Céline. And for good reason: They are completely different women. They all have different personalities, and the moments I built for them reflect that. Zendaya won the CFDA's coveted Fashion Icon Award at just twenty-five years old, and two years before that, Céline Dion was championed by *Vanity Fair* as a fashion icon at the age of forty-nine, both as the result of our work together. Which brings me to a lesson that I'll never forget: the power of starting over. It's something I'm living through right now.

When Céline Dion first reached out to me, I thought, *Céline who?* I hadn't dared to dream that big of a dream before—that this legend, this woman whose music we've sung for more than thirty years was calling to work with me.

I want to be clear: Céline had a rich and layered history, and all I did was help take a new lens to what was already there. We began working together in 2016. It was an incredibly sensitive time for the star. Her husband, the music producer and manager René Angélil, had recently passed away, as had her brother, Daniel Dion. She was ready for a new perspective. She had been in the public eye for thirty years since she first burst onto the Canadian music scene as a teen. But it was time for something different: It was time for Céline to not only be at the forefront of her own story, but to have fun.

Before our first meeting together, I embarked on a large amount of research to understand her style history. I looked at the designers she preferred for daytime, red carpet, and performances. I saw the silhouettes, the colors, the fabrics, and the vibes she leaned toward. And I began to see the ways that I could shake it up. I do this for every single person I work with—I can't build a new house without assessing the foundation. (Don't worry, in chapter 3 we will talk about how you can do the same in your own life.)

I brought racks and racks of clothing to her hotel in Paris so I could begin to see her preferences and the way she approached style. We spent eight hours together that day. We talked, we played with clothes, we laughed. I got a sense of who she is and what she is drawn to—outside of what we normally see from the polished, professional Céline. Yes, we all know she wore gowns to perform in Vegas. She was sophisticated, ladylike on the street. And while all those things are true to who she is, I could see there was something else.

Over the span of those meetings and conversations, I met a cool, young Céline who knew everything about fashion. I was exposed to all of these clothes she owned but was never photographed in. I saw binders full of tear sheets from magazines that had inspired her over the years. I found out that, contrary to what I was told by her team, she really didn't want to wear a scarf with every look. I met a risk taker who was at home in almost any garment and possessed the confidence to pull it all off. This was a side of this global star that I felt the world had never seen before. And that's the Céline I built my vision around.

For one of our fittings, I brought her an oversized Vetements hoodie printed with an image from *Titanic*. To be honest, it was a few seasons old at that point, and I had to write to the brand to see if they still had one in their archive for us to borrow or purchase. The hoodie obviously called back to her iconic performance of the film's theme song, so I was nervous when I showed it to her. I knew it would be a moment and I was confident in that, but we had only been working together for a few weeks—I wasn't sure if she'd like it or think it was too campy. The question was whether she would trust me enough to see the vision yet.

When she came in that day for her fitting at the Royal Monceau hotel in Paris, I didn't actually present the hoodie to her. I laid it out on the table and just left it there in a room full of racks of clothes and shoes. She walked in, and I'll never forget: she said, "What is this?"

I explained that it was from the French brand Vetements, which was a new fashion house at the time. And she just asked, "Are we wearing this today?" I told her we could! There was no animosity or condescension from this global megastar. It was just pure curiosity and the willingness to try. It was trust, to be honest. Trust of me, trust of the process, trust of the vision. We paired it with skinny jeans, gold Gucci heels, and a little Gucci bag.

Céline has this thing. When she puts on clothes that she really likes, her posture, her walk, everything just changes. That's a testament to how transformative clothing can be. It can happen with anyone. Everything just becomes a little taller, a little more refined. With Céline, she would get this slight wiggle in her walk. It's a sort of *you can't tell me nothing* type of vibe. So when we put it all on that day with the jewelry and did the final little touches, she looked at herself again. And then I saw it: that strut, that wiggle.

Before meeting her, I never would have thought she could pull something like that off. I didn't even think she would be interested in the hoodie. But getting to know her, I saw something else. I'm so happy she proved my initial thought wrong. When we went downstairs, I did one more look-over to make sure everything was just as perfect as she felt, and then she was gone into the blinding light of photographers on

> # The key is to never be afraid to prove everyone wrong: it's never too late to start over.

the street and hordes of her screaming fans.

That was one of the first outfits we did together—the look heard round the world—and it changed the perception of Céline Dion, which is not easy to do for someone who has been a star for so long. *Vanity Fair* said it was the moment she stepped "into her new status as a bona fide style icon" at the age of forty-nine. From there, she began to lean into this new energy, later saying in interviews she felt like she was just starting her life at fifty.

"[Law] brought me out of my closet and now flowers are growing," she told *ET's* Carly Steel that year. That's the point of all of my work, to reignite and invigorate the people I work with. To help give them permission to be themselves more authentically and without compromise. And to do that for a legend like Céline has been humbling.

The experience with Céline was no doubt in the back of my mind when I posted my retirement to Instagram. For a decade I had been "Law Roach, the stylist" or "Law Roach, the Image Architect." As all of the comments on the Instagram post told me, no one could or would see me any other way. But there are other sides of me, as there were to Céline, and as there are to you.

The key is to never be afraid to prove everyone wrong: it's never too late to start over.

"Perhaps the greatest risk any of us will ever take is to be seen as we really are."

—FAIRY GODMOTHER, *CINDERELLA* (2015)

O2.

ASSESSING YOUR
FOUNDATIONS

O n a chilly Monday night in November 2022, I found myself sitting in Cipriani's, on the southernmost tip of Manhattan.

The elegant Kerry Washington was on the stage, looking radiant in a ruffled black Vera Wang blazer and a bold red lip. She was smiling as she said to the gathered crowd: "Once upon a time, there was a queen born on the South Side of Chicago."

The room was silent as she continued, with only the occasional burst of applause interrupting. "A queen who was a fierce force for good and for beauty. And she changed the landscape of fashion just by being her. Tonight, ladies and gentlemen, I have the distinct honor of presenting the inaugural CFDA Stylist Award to my dear friend, collaborator, and queen mother Law Roach." Kerry continued and I listened to her talk about my work, about our experiences together, and I felt the tears spring to my eyes.

She talked about when we had first worked together years earlier, when she was less comfortable and confident on red carpets. Kerry talked about what's really at the core of what I do. "Law saw in me something different. Something raw. More true. And he challenged me and guided me to stop dropping the persona and become more of myself on the carpet and in my life." Her speaking about this so publicly brought a tear to my eye.

She continued: "It doesn't matter whether it's for editorial or for press or for carpets or for life, Law's process is exceptional. He doesn't put together an outfit. He's determined to create a masterpiece, one detail at a time. He builds artful fashion moments, memories, tableaus, narratives. The clothes, the glam, the look. It's all a story, and he is our showrunner."

She went on: "I have learned so much from you. You don't follow the rules. You don't play anybody else's game. You are uncompromisingly and unapologetically yourself. You know exactly who you are.

You know exactly what you want. You are intentional. You are brilliant."

The CFDA Fashion Awards celebrate the most outstanding contributions and achievements in the fashion industry, and they are a level of recognition that is unparalleled within the business. On this magical night, I was the first-ever recipient of the Stylist Award. Kerry called the event my coronation, and it truly felt like it was.

It was surreal to be surrounded by the industry's best designers, most lauded stylists, entertainers, actors, and fashion insiders, all listening raptly to Ms. Washington, who had playfully doted on me moments earlier on the red carpet as if she was the stylist and I was the star. I felt so seen for my work and my vision. I felt celebrated in a room full of the people that I had admired and respected for so long. I was in awe.

Then it was my turn to take the stage and face this room, and in some ways, face myself. *How did I get here?* Here I was, Lawrence Roach from Chicago, in head-to-toe Oscar de la Renta, taking the stage to the applause of so many of the fashion icons I admired.

I walked toward that stage, clutching my floor-length, white polka dot ensemble to avoid tripping. The look itself was historic: de la Renta had never made a men's look before, and I was honored that the incredible designers Fernando Garcia and Laura Kim wanted me to be the first to wear one. I like to say that I was making history on top of history that night.

I embraced Kerry and stood behind the podium feeling absolutely overcome with joy, pride, and of course, nerves. I didn't prepare a speech; I spoke from the heart. Speaking in front of that room— including and especially Anna Wintour—was intimidating. I took a deep breath and triggered my confidence.

Looking out into the sea of people applauding and honoring my years of work was humbling and awe-inspiring. To be recognized for my ability to see my clients for who they are, to empower them and support them in owning their truest selves and flaunting it in editorials and on red carpets in the most outrageous and beautiful ways possible, was all I could have asked for.

One of the things I said in that moment sticks with me today. I told the audience: "I wasn't promised this life. I didn't even grow up wanting this life. I think this life chose me. I really believe that the universe gives you exactly what you need when you're supposed to have it."

And while that's all true, the only reason any of it was possible was because I've always known who I am and have been unshakeable in those beliefs.

ONCE UPON A TIME

We all come from somewhere, and that somewhere has a huge impact on our lives.

For me, I grew up in Chicago, moving around the South Side of the city, mostly near Seventy-Ninth Street and Essex in the South Shore. I have four younger siblings, and we were raised by my mother.

It wasn't an easy life. I was a really feminine boy who grew up in a neighborhood that was just as tough as I was feminine. If you've ever heard my voice, I've had the same voice all my life. I never tried to deepen it or change that. My mannerisms have also always been a little flamboyant. And while I was wearing Air Force 1s and baggy Girbaud jeans, I wasn't trying to mask who I was; my teenage years were the time of Da Brat and TLC. Everyone dressed like boys, even the girls. So that's how I expressed my own femininity. This all meant that there was a little bit of bullying—I knew then, and I know now, it could have been much, much worse—but it didn't deter me.

Even then, I knew who I was and I never apologized for it. I think it was probably because of the men in my family. Growing up I had many strong masculine influences, including my grandfather and five uncles who all accepted me as I was. That base of love gave me my initial confidence, and ultimately, it was that confidence that made others accept who I was without much incident.

When I think back on it, I never really had a "coming out" moment. I remember, in my twenties, listening to friends swap stories of when they decided to speak their truth to the world in these pivotal life events, and I realized I never had that experience. I lived as my truest and most authentic self from a very young age, without asking anyone for permission to do so. There was never a big moment of reveal because I lived out who I was day in and day out; what's understood never needs to be explained. I never had to explain myself to anybody. There was no hiding who I am, and I never tried to.

> I lived as my truest and most authentic self from a very young age, without asking anyone for permission to do so.

The city of Chicago shaped me. There's an ethos there. I come from a family of loudmouths and a culture of showboating. The whole neighborhood wanted to stunt and wear their best and flashiest at any given opportunity. It was a type of peacocking; that cultural "look at me" that my people do so well. We don't call it this anymore, but it was about looking fly at any and all costs. It was about proclaiming who you were at every opportunity and not taking shit from anybody.

If that didn't prepare me for life in Hollywood, I don't know what did! I've always had a little bit of that in me, that ability to hold my own in a high-pressure setting.

Much of it starts with my mother. My mom was a hustler. She had this ability to read situations and adapt accordingly. She knew how to be exactly who she needed to be to survive. At some of our lowest moments, when we didn't have money for food, my mother could go to the grocery store and read people's body language before interacting with them. Each time she would leave with her groceries paid for. I spent my childhood observing that, seeing her change like a chameleon to best fit different circumstances to get what she wanted out of life. She knew how to become just who she needed to be in the exact moment that she had to in order to make someone her ally.

I saw how she took particular care in getting dressed for the day, in styling her hair and applying makeup. It's not that she was high maintenance, it's more that she honored herself. She also understood that, at the end of the day, clothes are tools of communication.

My extended family had a big presence in my upbringing, my grandmother especially. I watched how intentional she was before going out into the world as well: the night before an important event, she would press and lay out what she was going to wear and put her hair in rollers. Then when morning came, I would sit at her feet as she put it all on, watching her transform into the confident woman the world would see. It was like magic in front of my eyes. I think I became addicted to that magic, and it has led to what I do today.

My grandmother would inspire me in many ways, including igniting my love for vintage clothing. Every Sunday after church and before dinner we would go "junking," as she used to call it. To her that meant going to thrift stores to find treasures to take home. For her, the draw was knickknacks more than clothes. She could always be convinced to bring little novelty salt and pepper shakers home. While she was doing that, I would wander around the store and watch women try on hats and belts. I would watch them style entire looks from pieces others had disposed of as trash.

All of these experiences shaped the person that I am. That unconditional love from others established a foundation of confidence in me that has always been present, even when I was heavier and felt uncomfortable in my body. Having the skills of using my clothes to both affirm myself and communicate to others what I learned from my mother and grandmother means I've always been able to walk in a room and exude confidence to the point of turning heads, making people wonder, *Who is he?* Even when I had no money and no success, that was there.

I've always had an undercurrent of confidence, of knowing who I am and that I'll figure out whatever situation I find myself in. That confidence is such a blessing. It feels divine sometimes—and I do believe parts of it are inexplicable. I've embraced it, and even from a young age, it was something I knew that I needed to share with others. I've always tried to raise up the people around me, to instill confidence and reflect back to people what makes each of them so great. That mirror is especially important, as it can help them establish their own confidence and carry it with them wherever they go.

If I can get a little vulnerable for a moment, the only real dip in my confidence happened recently. After my retirement—which was controversial for so many who didn't understand why someone would go out in a moment of success—I found myself questioning what to do next. But then I got hold of myself: I did it before, and I can do it again.

And so can you. Let's talk about how.

BUILDING LUXURY LAW

You probably don't know this, but I have a bachelor's in psychology and a master's in business administration with a concentration in marketing. Yes, two degrees. It's true. But not long after I graduated, my mother passed away. In the wake of that tragedy, my two younger brothers, who were still living with her, found themselves without a guardian. So I stepped in to help raise them. It wasn't cheap.

I needed to make money to support myself and my brothers, so I got a job bartending at a big club in Chicago. If I'm being honest, I was *really good* at it. I had the natural confidence to hold my own behind the bar with a rowdy crowd, and I was likable, so people wanted to pull up a barstool, chat, and of course, tip me. Those moments of watching my mother size up people for her own benefit paid off; being behind that bar put food on the table.

But it wasn't the healthiest lifestyle. I was drinking a lot; bartenders have to be part of the party. I was also staying out way too late, having a few drinks, and going out to eat after the bar closed. I wasn't looking my best, and I wasn't feeling it, either.

I could have found a corporate job—something that paid six figures, included benefits, and put my degrees to work in a more direct way—but something kept telling me not to. If I had gone that route back then I probably would have had a decent life. Comfortable, even. But I don't know if I would have been happy. The reason I had gotten my master's in business administration was because a cousin of mine had landed a six-figure job after getting the same degree. I found out later that she hated it. I already had the degree by that point, but I knew I didn't want the same life she had.

So I held out for dreams of something bigger. I had always loved clothes and fashion. When I was younger, I would tell anyone who would listen that I wanted to be a fashion designer, the way many young kids do. At around seven years old, I made a little book of sketches with my own notes about clothes. One of my uncles had a girlfriend named Marilyn, and she bought that book from me for five dollars to show how much she believed in me. She believed in that dream, and that was all the permission I needed.

Subconsciously that's what I think I was waiting for: something that connected my love for clothes and fashion with my desire to inspire confidence in others. And I wasn't going to get tied up in anything else lest my dreams never come true. I wasn't ready to give up— no one should, you included.

It's funny that even though I felt so strongly about resisting the temptation of a regular nine to five job, at that point, I didn't have specific dreams for my future. I certainly couldn't have known what was to come. But in my mind, I didn't have to know. I trusted myself. I trusted my abilities. I knew it would work out. I held onto the feeling that something big was out there for me and was confident that when the opportunity presented itself, I would be ready. And I was.

It was around this time that I started to get more interested in buying and selling vintage clothes. My interest came from those Sunday afternoon "junking" trips with my grandmother, and it turned out to be useful; though I was making good money, I didn't really have the cash to buy designer labels. The first designer shoes I purchased were a pair of brown Gucci brogues by Tom Ford with the Gucci buckle across the front. The $375 price tag felt like thousands of dollars. But I had an eye for finding diamonds in the rough, and I could pick out the perfect vintage pieces that made a style statement. I started going regularly to vintage shops and searching for pieces for myself. My friends noticed and started making requests. Through word of mouth, that circle began to spread wider.

I spent a year or two collecting and curating exceptional pieces for myself and for anyone who requested them. I kept my collection in the trunk of my car. It grew bigger than I realized it could, and I attracted such a large following that women were coming to see its contents in droves. The trunk became way too small for the size of my operation.

In 2006, I decided to open a vintage boutique on Halsted at Eighteenth Street in East Pilsen with my friend Siobhan Strong, whom I'd known since childhood. We called it Deliciously Vintage.

Running a business is not for the faint of heart. We weren't making a ton of money, but it gave us purpose. We were renting this huge space with provincial French furniture and pink and black striped walls. One wall eventually became a local photo op for those visiting or passing by the store; at the monthly art walk, people would come in for cocktails and then snap photos for social media. The boutique gave me a little bit of status. It was something to be known for in the hustle and bustle of Chicago. And it introduced me to a community of people who would become important to my career and my life.

What made us stand out was that each item in the store was hand-picked by Siobhan or me. We would scour estate sales and anywhere else we could to source pieces, selecting items that we knew would sell. In the store, we organized pieces by trend and color to spark inspiration in customers. Our collection included a range of designers and sizes; we wanted to make it really appealing to all women. You could find Dior and Saint Laurent next to a designer whose name you had never heard of that was stitched into the label of a look you *had* to have. And I wasn't above adding a few tweaks either; if I thought changing a hemline or putting in a new waist would make something more modern, that's what we did.

Our biggest break in gaining a national spotlight was in 2009 when Kanye West stopped by to shop for his then-girlfriend Amber Rose. The press picked up on his visit, and it helped put us on the map.

I was a workaholic. I was styling clients here and there, in addition to running Deliciously Vintage. It was a natural next step to go from helping select pieces and styling them in the store to pulling entire looks for events. At first, some Chicago-based actors and models got in touch with us or came by the store for us to dress them for events. Our first styling clients were *America's Next Top Model*'s Eva Marcille and *Prison Break*'s Rockmond Dunbar. Then it snowballed.

I started getting some work in New York City. Sometimes I would tell little lies to ease the process. If a possible client reached out about some work that needed to happen in Manhattan and they asked where I was based, I told them that I was based there. And I was (on the days they needed me to be). Nothing was going to stand in my way, especially not a two-hour-and-fifteen-minute flight. I ended up doing a few jobs for people like Swizz Beats and K. Michelle.

When I decided that I was going to pursue a career as a stylist, I was determined to put everything I had into it.

While running Deliciously Vintage, I met a woman I call Godmother Eunice. She came from Houston and would often tell me stories of the circles she ran in, which often overlapped with those of Tina Knowles. (As she would tell me, Godmother Eunice would often go out to social events knowing she was the sharpest, best-dressed woman in the room. And she would be, at least until Ms. Tina walked in.) One day, while we were talking in the shop and I was sharing with her what was going on in my life, she stopped me. "Can I give you some advice?" she asked.

"Sure," I said nervously.

"Do you really want to do this type of thing?" she asked, looking around the store. At the time I had the store, I had my growing styling gigs, and I was still behind the bar every weekend to make sure the bills were paid.

"Yes, I really do. I love it," I responded.

"Well, you're never going to win the game if you're not in the stadium. Why are you still here in Chicago? Is this where you're going to win the game?"

Her statement stopped me in my tracks. It made me really question myself. What was I doing? Why was I still in Chicago? I was no longer taking care of my brothers. And here was someone who I knew had my best interest at heart and who was a successful businesswoman encouraging me to go all in.

So I did. I quit my job at the bar. I quit drinking. I took about six weeks to myself in Chicago and worked on getting my health on track. And then I took the plunge. I moved to Los Angeles and got into the stadium just like Godmother Eunice said.

When I decided that I was going to pursue a career as a stylist, I was determined to put everything I had into it. I knew that I wanted to be the best at whatever I set out to do. But I had no idea how that was going to happen.

IDENTITY: WHO ARE YOU AND WHAT DO YOU WANT?

Before any architect begins building, you must assess the project at hand. You need to consider your goals and then make plans—a blueprint, if you will. You decide what's most important.

Before you start thinking of any of the clothes that you think will make you a fashion icon, it's important to understand that the clothing is just a form of communication. You're talking to the world without opening your mouth. So just like you wouldn't speak without having thoughts or a point of view, a fashion icon doesn't get dressed without those things, either.

We will begin to talk about the clothes in the next chapter, but it's important that we first get a sense of who you are. Get clear on your vision for your life and who you want to be in the world. Knowing yourself will help secure your own self-confidence, which will allow you to wear just about anything you want from there.

Here are some steps to help you start the conversation with yourself:

- **Reflect on Your Values:** Consider what matters most to you. When you lay your head down on your pillow each night, consider what you're most proud of from the day. Understanding your core values will help you make decisions and act in a way that aligns with what truly matters to you. For me, it's important to be seen as I see myself. It's important to be authentic and to live life on my own terms. You can see that in every aspect of my life, from my professional life to the clothes I wear. Do you value that too? Or do you value the ability to blend in?

- **Identify Your Passions:** Think about the activities, interests, and topics that ignite your enthusiasm. What could you spend hours doing without feeling bored or tired? Your passions often hold clues to what you want to pursue in your life. I've always enjoyed helping people, teaching others, encouraging them, and working on projects together. Especially when there's a creative aspect, I can get so wrapped up in my work that I forget to eat.

- **Define Your Goals:** Set both short-term and long-term goals that relate to your career, personal growth, relationships, or other areas of life. Not all goals are created equal, darling. Prioritize them based on what's most important to you right now so you can focus your energy on what truly matters.

- **Imagine Your Ideal Future:** Visualize where you want to be in the future. What does your ideal life look like in five years, ten years, or twenty years? Consider various aspects of your life, such as your career, relationships, health, and personal development. For my career, I knew I wanted to build a career similar to that of Rachel Zoe's. She provided me with a snapshot of what my future might look like. Feel free to take inspiration from those around you or people who you admire. But at the end of the day, you have to create a future that is in alignment with your goals.

- **Set Priorities:** Not everything can be pursued at once. Prioritize your goals and aspirations to create a clear path forward. Determine what steps you need to take to move closer to your vision. To pursue my vision of taking a styling career seriously in Los Angeles, I knew that I needed to get my personal life in order. That's often the case: before you pursue something outwardly, you must do an internal adjustment to prepare yourself. What do you need to do to get to your next step?

Remember, this is a dynamic process that can evolve over time as you learn and grow. Stay committed to your values and passions while remaining open to new opportunities and experiences.

Style is a way of presenting yourself to the world, and it can help you to remind yourself of a few things. When you do it right by your

own definition of success, you can express and affirm your best and
most authentic self. But first you must get clear on your vision for
your life and who you want to be.

LET YOUR LIGHT SHINE

In 2011, I was running Deliciously Vintage and styling a few clients in
New York and LA when I got a call that would change my life.

A woman (who later would become my Big Sister and Mentor,
Chasity) who was a regular client of the store called about a favor for
her friend's daughter. This fourteen-year-old girl was a young actress,
known for her roles on the Disney Channel. My client told me that
this actress had been invited to Justin Bieber's *Never Say Never* premiere and she didn't have anything to wear. It was a big red carpet
moment for her and an opportunity to stand out. My client suggested
that the two of us go shopping together. Next thing I knew, I had disappeared into the Kitson boutique at Santa Monica Place with a teenage Zendaya.

Zendaya has always had a love for fashion. Before we worked
together, she would style herself for red carpets. She remembers vividly the first day we met. I was carrying a YSL bag that she recognized
and asked me about. To have a teenager who was already so clued in
to designers and trends, who also possessed a movie-star level of charisma, was refreshing.

Needless to say, we became fast friends. I remember how much
she listened to what I was saying that first day. She was so eager to
learn and genuinely invested. Someone with those qualities who is
also naturally beautiful is rare in this business. And I knew then I was
lucky to have met her.

For that first event, I helped Z select a silver metallic blazer paired
with a shiny gray miniskirt featuring a zipper down the middle. It
was a very 2011 look that we may now look back on and regret, but

it was a product of the time. Actually, back then in the mall she was understandably hesitant. It might not seem like a big deal, but the skirt was shiny and eye-catching. She thought it might be risky. This was a teen with a lot of eyes on her, trying out a style that was new to her. She worried about what people would think—what they would say and write about her if they didn't like what she was wearing. In response, I put my hands on her shoulders and said as gently as I possibly could: "Who gives a fuck?" If she liked it, that's all that mattered. I said it in the same way that I would have to any of my younger siblings. And that's how I thought of her—like a little sister.

I didn't have to say anything else about it. I didn't need to explain what I meant. I saw the shift in her at that very moment. She didn't repeat it out loud, but I'm pretty sure she repeated it in her teenage head.

Days later, Zendaya was beaming on that red carpet. She was working the blazer, and it was clear that she felt confident. It didn't matter what people said so long as she felt beautiful in the outfit. Sure, it wasn't one of those moments that was chronicled in the pages of the fashion establishment, but in that moment, I can tell you a fashion icon was born. She knew who she was and dressed to communicate that. Her confidence reverberated through anyone who caught a glimpse of her. Even if the rest of the world didn't recognize it yet, she was iconic. But it wasn't just a moment for her; it was also a major moment for me.

Some things are just meant to be. Some people come into our lives at just the right time. For me, Zendaya was the inspiration, the muse, and the push I needed to jump into styling full speed ahead. Though I had been committed to it before, Z became the perfect close collaborator to do the work I knew I was capable of.

When I first started working with Zendaya, she was young and a "Disney girl" who wasn't being taken seriously by major fashion designers. I was just starting out as a stylist, but I hadn't come up through "the system." Most stylists spend a year or even a few years as an intern before assisting for a few more years. That's how they make connections and build relationships. That's how they learn the "rules" of how to do things and build an exchange of doing favors for one another. I didn't have any of that. I didn't know the rules of what you should and shouldn't do. All I had was my belief in this girl. She wanted to be a fashion star, and I knew she could do it. She was beautiful, and the world needed to know about her.

My plan for Zendaya was for her to be a chameleon. The celebrity fashion market was crowded, with every girl being known for a signature look (which allowed them to be easily matched up to a specific stylist known for having a similar aesthetic). I decided that we would go against that: Zendaya would be the ultimate fashion icon, able to wear any look, anywhere. In the early days that meant being a little aggressive: I would scour the looks other celebs had worn and then put them on Zendaya, which would make it into the then-famous "Who Wore It Best" columns. I'll let you guess who typically won.

I didn't know the rules of what you should and shouldn't do. All I had was my belief in this girl.

Z's appearance was always being switched up: a new style, a new cut, a new color. At one event, she would arrive with really long hair to her knees, and the next day, she'd be sporting a chic bob. One day it could be an Alice & Olivia animal print minidress; the next a shocking-pink Ungaro two-piece. You never knew what to expect from her, and she wasn't afraid to take risks because she had a bedrock of confidence that she could always pull any outfit off.

If fashion is a tool of communication, Z was going to be a polyglot: she could speak any language fluently. And each one was her native tongue.

My little sister in fashion was also showing up to places where she didn't belong. She'd be walking the red carpet at the Grammy Awards, where pundits would question why she was there. But I knew that being on the red carpet would be the way to elevate her entire career. She was there to pull a look! That's the only excuse she ever needed. And when those garments started doing the talking, every major fashion outlet was listening.

It's not easy to be a fifteen-year-old Disney star showing up at the Grammys on the red carpet with some of the greatest style icons, like Beyoncé and Lady Gaga. Anyone could be crushed by the attention in that environment if they didn't have rock-solid self-confidence. But Zendaya rose to the occasion time after time. She would walk the carpet and be photographed like she belonged there. And she did.

All of this was happening as Instagram was first gaining massive popularity, and so much of the cultural conversation on social media revolved around visuals. Z's gorgeous photographs played well in that medium and won her many new fans.

This might sound like I'm puffing, but the proof is there. Back at the 2015 Oscars red carpet, I put Z in a perfectly delicate, off-the-shoulder white satin gown from Vivienne Westwood. She wasn't nominated for a movie or there to present; she was just there to look fab. (She later admitted that she wasn't even really invited—an agent had an extra ticket and from there, she snuck onto the red carpet.) As a team, we decided that the ideal way to complete the look would be to style her hair in dreadlocks. We thought it was fitting and glamorous. The night of the event, in a now infamous quote on *The Fashion Police*, Giuliana Rancic said she thought it made Z look as if she smelled of "patchouli oil" and "weed." So Zendaya, at the tender age of eighteen, broke it down for her.

"There is a fine line between what is funny and disrespectful," she wrote on Instagram. "Someone said something about my hair at the Oscars that left me in awe. Not because I was relishing in rave outfit reviews, but because I was hit with ignorant slurs and pure disrespect." In the open letter, she name-checked other massively successful Black people with locs—Ava DuVernay, Ledisi, Terry McMillan, and more—in addition to her father, brother, and cousins.

"My wearing my hair in locs on an Oscars red carpet was to show-case them in a positive light, to remind people of color that our hair is good enough," she continued. "To me locs are a symbol of strength and beauty, almost like a lion's mane. I suggest some people should listen to India Arie's 'I Am Not My Hair' and contemplate a little before opening your mouth so quickly to judge."

That was the message of the look, whether she had to speak it with her mouth or not. I look back often and think of how poised and professional she was at just eighteen. Everyone wanted to interview her at that moment, but she declined them all. The restraint she showed spoke to her own maturity. But what we were doing wasn't just clothes: Z and I were having an open dialogue with our people from the red carpet of the Oscars. And every day, you can be starting a conversation from wherever you happen to be.

In the years since I started working with Z, I've pushed her toward embracing her confidence and a give-no-fucks attitude. I've had the privilege of watching her blossom into the fashion industry's hottest star and most authentic, fearless risk taker.

"You have taught me so much about myself," Z said to me at the 2019 InStyle Awards. "You taught me to be more confident. To not give an F about what people think, to allow myself to be proud of who I am when I step outside and when I look in the mirror. You always remind me if I ever get nervous about my hair, makeup, or whatever, that—do you care what they really think? And I say nope, and then we go."

After almost thirteen years of working together, we celebrated a huge moment when Zendaya was named Fashion Icon at the 2021 CFDA awards in November 2021. Z was joining a list of Fashion Icon recipients that included Naomi Campbell, Rihanna, Jennifer Lopez, and many other heavy hitters in the fashion world. It was incredible knowing Zendaya was making history as the youngest person to ever receive the title.

For Zendaya and me, this moment solidified our hard work. It was a testament to our countless looks and experiments, tried-and-true friendship, and mutual trust.

I went to the CFDA awards with her. Z wore a custom two-piece Vera Wang design in a bright, hot red color. I also wore a custom Vera Wang. She put together this incredible plaid outfit for me with my name embroidered on the sleeve. Z and I both wore our hair in long braids. It was a small visual cue of the fashion siblings we are.

Letting your light shine is stepping into the spotlight of your own life's stage. It's what Zendaya did when she put powerful words behind the image we had created together for her on the Oscars red carpet, allowing her to control her narrative. It's what I did when I didn't let anyone deter me from being the feminine boy that I was growing up. It's ultimately what Kerry Washington was thanking me for helping her do on stage at the CFDA awards.

And just like any of us, you deserve to be center stage of your own life. (That's what Godmother Eunice was encouraging me to do back in Chicago—to stop pursuing my dream as a side hustle and make it my focal point by moving to Los Angeles.) You deserve to embrace your authentic self, unapologetically, and without reservation.

It's about not dimming your radiance for anyone else's comfort or expectations. Whether you're pursuing your dream career, making a bold fashion choice, or speaking your truth, doing it with confidence and grace, without fear of judgment or the need for approval, is the only way. Letting your light shine means being the star of your own show and living your life on your terms. That's the way your dreams will be unlocked. Just like mine.

"Don't wait on anyone to tell you what you are worth. You have to be the first person who knows what you are worth and can say what you are worth."

—CLEO WADE, *HEART TALK: POETIC WISDOM FOR A BETTER LIFE*

O3.

CRAFTING YOUR STYLE STORY

n February 2021, a full year after the world shut down for COVID, people were still very cautious about being outside. But as it always does in Hollywood, the show went on.

For the first time, red carpet season happened virtually, with stars video chatting their acceptance speeches and manufacturing red carpet moments on Instagram through photoshoots. At the time, I was working with the actress Anya Taylor-Joy, who had just starred in *The Queen's Gambit* on Netflix. We had begun to work together more than a year prior, and I remember the moment I could see the fashion icon in her: for a premiere of her film *Emma*, I put her in a vintage Bob Mackie gown inspired by Audrey Hepburn in *My Fair Lady* and watched her come alive. My vision of her as this young, sophisticated debutante who could have easily been from the 1950s or 1960s came to life. She was a modern-day princess to me, and since *The Queen's Gambit* was set during the fifties and sixties, this vintage visual narrative was perfect for her awards-season campaign.

I don't just create looks. I create moments.

For the Golden Globes, I put her in an emerald-green custom Christian Dior haute couture gown. It shimmered when the light hit it and came with a long duster coat that added to its regalness. Watching Anya walk around the ballroom for our shoot, it was clear that she felt every bit of her youthful elegance. Even in our second option for the night, another Dior design by Maria Grazia Chiuri with a sculpted bodice, you could feel the young, innocent effervescence radiating from her as she twirled on her Instagram. It was something that translated even through your phone.

In another post, we re-created that iconic jewelry box scene from *Pretty Woman*. I was the Richard Gere to Anya's Julia Roberts, snapping a box of Tiffany & Co. jewelry closed on her fingers. *She* was the prettiest woman that night.

That awards season, Anya was one of the buzziest new Hollywood names. And that night at the Golden Globe Awards, this beauty, surrounded with an air of old school glamour I helped to conjure, walked away with the trophy. While I would never take any credit for her award—Anya is one of the most incisive actors of her generation and I have nothing to do with that—giving the viewers at home this pitch-perfect visual trajectory of her career was something we were very intentional about. It was something we constructed together.

It's the intricate type of work that you can easily implement into your own process each day.

THE ART OF STORYTELLING

I don't just create looks. I create moments.

At the end of the day, I am a storyteller. Yes, the language is different from what you may typically think when you hear the label (clothes are the words I use to convey my message and evoke a response from the observer), but I'm still telling a story. When I work with anyone—whether it's for editorial, for an event, or for a red carpet—there has to be some type of narrative. I have to know what I'm trying to say before I approach the wardrobe. I just use the clothes to express that.

Storytelling lies at the heart of *everything* we all do, from posts on social media, to presenting our professional ideas, to connecting with friends. We're all storytellers. Doesn't every good brunch start with "*Girl* . . ." before someone launches into a dramatic retelling of what's going on in their life? The way you present yourself to the world is one way that you choose to tell your story.

I've always known that style is one of the strongest forms of self-expression we have at our disposal. It's a language we all speak, whether we realize it or not. When spoken with purpose, it can have a powerful impact on our lives. Truly owning the clothes and the story they tell is important for those wearing them. It's what separates the icons from . . . well, everyone else.

Think of your style as your visual personality. It's the way you show up in the world, so understanding the energies and vibes that are core to your personality is a huge part of the process. This works in two ways: Style isn't just about communicating things to others; it can also be used to communicate or affirm things within yourself. No matter what someone else may think of a piece on the hanger, if you feel something when you put it on, it will transmit to everyone else when you wear it.

When I'm in a fitting with a client, it's often not about which dress is prettiest, or which pair of pants provides the perfect fit. It's about which pieces give them some type of emotion. Maybe an outfit gives them that extra bump of confidence they need to get through the day, maybe it makes them feel ten times more regal, or maybe it gives the that kick of drama they need to demand attention. I look for that take-your-breath-away moment—and it doesn't always come from the clothes you'd expect.

That was certainly the feeling I had when I dressed one-of-a-kind actress Hunter Schafer for the 2023 *Vanity Fair* Oscar Party. Hunter is a model and one of the most stunning people on the planet. After a successful career as a model, she really broke ground with her role on HBO's *Euphoria*, and she was quickly one of the hot young people to watch on red carpets. We started working together in late 2020.

I had seen a very special look during Paris Fashion Week a few weeks before the *Vanity Fair* party on the runway at the Ann Demeulemeester show. The outfit was a bias-cut white silk skirt paired with a single ivory-colored feather on top. I immediately thought of

Hunter. There was something daring and completely unique about it. And ultimately, I knew it would be beautiful on the right person who also possessed the body confidence to pull it off. I've never seen something more perfect for somebody.

For Hunter, because she's a model, she knows how to pose her body and work with any outfit. You'll notice that her pose in photos is always perfect for what she's wearing. That night, she showed off the cut of the skirt with the angles of her hip. I'll be honest: there was not a lot of fabric, but Hunter knew exactly how to stand to make it look flawless.

The decision for Hunter to wear this look was something that took a little while. And that's totally understandable. We had another amazing option from Alexander McQueen, and it wasn't until the last minute that she decided what she would wear. Amongst ourselves we called the Demeulemeester "the titties" look to differentiate it from the rest. I know better than to push someone into wearing this kind of outfit if they aren't ready. That confidence has to come from within.

Sometimes that happens. You see something that you think might work, but you're a little unsure about it. Maybe thoughts of what others might think creep in. Or maybe you aren't confident you can pull it off. It may take a little time and coming back to the piece day after day before you've convinced yourself you're ready. But when you do, it will be something to behold.

"I think I'm going to go with 'the titties,'" Hunter told me over the phone in the days before the party. I found out later that she had texted Zendaya for advice, and she confirmed that "the titties" was the right way to go. We also spoke on the phone right before she hit the red carpet. I had called to do a last-minute check-in to make sure she didn't have second thoughts. I knew that without absolute confidence on her part, it could have been a complete disaster. "No, I'm good," she told me. "I'm ready."

When I saw the video footage of Hunter on the red carpet, I was so proud. She walked to the center of the carpet and took a beat to set herself up before the cameras. She pushed her hair back behind her shoulders, got her hips set just so, and worked the room like only she can. She held herself with perfect posture, held her head high, and owned the most daring look of the night.

This is all part of Hunter's story, owning her body and her power. It's a skill and strength of hers, and this look was the perfect way to show that off because it blended with the almost otherworldly beauty she possesses. If you've seen her, you know Hunter has this sort of fantastical, almost nymph-like appeal. Her beauty is distinct, with a sort of mystical element. The Demeulemeester ensemble encompassed all of that. Those attributes aren't always something that someone can consciously explain to you—there's a chance fans of this look couldn't tell you why they love it. But on a gut level they just know it works.

It was only fitting that the full collection that the look came from was about self-authorship. That wasn't just a feather on Hunter's chest, it was a quill. It was a symbol of her writing her own story and being in control of her own narrative, all of which has always been important to her coming up in this industry.

In general, you have to have a certain amount of confidence to stand on the red carpet in front of people screaming your name. It's not easy to face the flashing bulbs of the photographers' cameras, the microphones being thrust in your face, the noise, the chaos, the lights. It's all a lot to take in while you're trying to stand straight, smooth your skirt, and smile. Not to mention rubbing elbows with some of the biggest celebrities in Hollywood. Confidence is what will allow you to stand under the scrutiny of the entire world.

It helps, of course, to know that you look your best. There really must be no doubt that you have the best hair, the best makeup, the best accessories, and the best dress. You need to feel that you're your best self at that moment.

In Hunter's case, she was standing in front of all of those cameras just about next to naked. I wasn't there. *Nobody* else was there. *She* was there. Alone. She had to be confident in herself, and confident in the moment that she was creating with this look. And believe me, people bought into what she was selling. *Elle*, *People*, and *W Magazine* raved about the look. CNN called it their "Look of the Week," describing it as "ethereal." In twenty-four hours, her own Instagram post of the look racked up more than 2 million likes, and Google searches of her name skyrocketed.

But not all of us are Hunter Schafer. Not all of us can slip on a daring look easily, even if it aligns with the person we are inside or that we want to be. We might be experiencing one too many nerves. One thing that can help in high-stakes or out-of-the-box moments like this is creating a narrative around the dress like Hunter did. Look at yourself and ask, "Who is the girl wearing this outfit?" Try stepping out of yourself and into an almost alter ego. It's somewhere between Sasha Fierce and your best self. Kerry Washington called her version "red carpet Kerry," which was a performative version of her own self, someone a little braver and a little fancier. You're still you, but you're wearing a cape. (Sometimes you can even use something to trigger this within yourself to get yourself started. Maybe when you wear this hairstyle or put on these shades, that's the little sign you need. For me, my long, bone-straight buss down is the thing that brings out my own personal Sasha Fierce.) It's about creating a feeling, selling the look through your movements and your poses. It can be easier to be bold, exude confidence, feel playful when you're doing so as a separate persona. *That's* not me, that's the alter ego. Over time you'll find yourself relying on the persona less and less.

One of the most inspiring forms of self-expression is found within the drag community. Drag queens are often a persona, or a character, with a backstory as well as an aesthetic and performance style that they've cultivated over time. Drag has become an emblem of showmanship, of self-expression, and of pure confidence.

I've always loved drag queens—how they build characters through their clothes, hair, and makeup choices. It's performance and style at the highest level. Drag queens often, of course, tell stories as part of their performances, through various means such as lip-syncing to songs with narrative lyrics, engaging in comedic monologues, or using visual cues in their outfits and makeup. Some drag performances might center around personal experiences, social issues, or political commentary, while others might tell fictional stories or use satire to convey messages. The storytelling aspect of drag adds depth and meaning to the entertainment, making it an engaging and impactful form of expression.

I recently had the pleasure of doing my own photoshoot in full drag. *Interview* magazine reached out to me to do a shoot a few months after my retirement announcement, and I knew we could do something out-of-the-box. *Interview* is one of those magazines where you can kind of push the boundaries a little bit. (Sometimes that context helps: If a space is known for pushing the boundaries or being edgy, it can lower the stakes for you to try something new. It's the reason no one expects Broadway singing at the local bar karaoke—this isn't the space.) The magazine originally hadn't come to me with a specific vision in mind, but they knew

> It can be easier to be bold, exude confidence, feel playful when you're doing so as a separate persona.

my work from the *Barbarella*-themed Zendaya cover we had collaborated on in 2021. They let me take the lead, and I decided to do something I had been thinking about for a while: drag.

I have always secretly wanted to be a bit shocking in the way that drag is. You know, doing something a bit unexpected from the norm. When someone thinks they know who you are, when they think they have you all figured out, and then you show them a version of you that disrupts that line of thinking—that has always intrigued me. Though my look has evolved over time as I embraced more eclectic and gender fluid styles, drag was further than I had ever gone before. It was a part of my story I had yet to tap into but wanted to. For me, part of the shoot was about reclaiming my confidence. As I told you, when I announced my retirement, I was a little shaken. I thought this might be a way of grounding myself again. And I was right: It was empowering to be the subject of a photo shoot, to be daring and put myself out there on my own terms.

The pictures turned out very playful and evocative. For inspiration I was thinking of the Zendaya *Barbarella* cover we did, but I was also thinking about Paris Hilton in the early 2000s. It was about exploring the most feminine version of myself. I wanted to feel like a siren. If you know me at all by now, you know I don't take myself too seriously. For some of the shots, I wore a very glam little black dress with a coat over it, a red wig styled and teased for volume with a headband, and some silky thick false lashes. I wore a black outfit with black leather gloves layered with diamonds, of course, and stilettos. The style of the shoot was very avant-garde, very edgy, and almost behind-the-scenes, with a few shots of me in my robe between looks.

My favorite look of the day was the most unexpected. But then again, if you know me, maybe it's the most obvious one of all. The idea came about organically while I was at the shoot. I was changing when one of my assistants noticed how great my ass looked in my fishnet stockings, and the lightbulb went off. I kept the fishnets on, added some heels, and grabbed this gorgeous short Rick Owens fur coat. I just started bouncing around, kind of jumping and playing on the bed. I had this story in my head about the youthful innocence of playing dress-up, which I could express most effectively through movement. And I knew enough to keep my face out of the shot—just in case any future offspring are scrolling through the Internet one day. (You're welcome, future children.)

I really love that picture, and the entire shoot. I see the inspirations behind the outfits and the spontaneity of that long day (and the fun my team and I had!) every time I come back to them. I finally felt like I was living again after so much work-related anxiety about clothes, and any sense of doubt that might have crossed my mind before the first click of the camera was long gone.

WHAT'S YOUR STORY?

When I think about style and confidence, I think about my mother's black dress. She wore it everywhere: to weddings and funerals, to important church services and big life events. Every time my mother put on that black dress, I knew she was in her element. Yes, that dress was beautiful, but its true gift was that it made my mom feel beautiful. Every single time, without fail. It was her superhero cape, her everyday armor.

Clothing is the first line of defense, and often the first way you present who you are to the world. Finding your own personal style is an exhilarating journey of self-expression and reinvention. It can also be a crutch you can lean on. You can use clothing to help remind you of who you are and alter your mood accordingly.

Being a fashion icon means being unafraid to give your clothes life. If you find something you love, you shouldn't wear it just once.

We all know the frustration of being in a fitting room and trying on dress after dress or sweater after sweater, having none of them fit quite right until, suddenly, we come across *the one*. Why, then, do so many of us feel averse to being seen or photographed in a particular item more than once? There's such power that comes from owning a piece of clothing and knowing how it's going to fit your body and knowing how you're going to feel when you put it on.

In my personal style, I love to mix more feminine pieces and items that are women's clothing. I think the first time I put on a skirt, it changed something fundamental about my style, and it made me take more risks moving forward. It's only been in the last few years that I have experimented more and more with my style. When I was younger, I would never shop from the women's section. It was Kanye West wearing a Celine blouse at Coachella in 2011 that really flipped a switch in my mind. From there I began to explore on my own. What I found when I started to wear more gender fluid pieces is I became more comfortable and confident in my own personal style.

Companies would send me clothing and accessories, and when I began to be photographed in women's clothing, I began to receive more gender fluid pieces. My absolute favorite is a long nylon skirt that Nike sent me. It's my own version of my mom's little black dress—something I feel so comfortable and confident in every time I put it on. It makes me feel like the best version of myself, like I'm pulled together without trying too hard. I pair it with my favorite white button-down and either sneakers or slides.

The classic white button-down is my other favorite piece. It can do no wrong, instantly lifting a basic outfit into chic and pulled together. I'll let you in on a secret: I buy mine from Amazon. No joke. I order the same twelve-dollar shirt in bulk so I always have a few when I travel, or at the ready when I need to throw one on. They're forgiving, no matter if my weight is a little up or a little down.

I often pair the two together, and I have a favorite way of styling it to create a cohesive look. Instead of buttoning the shirt, I cross one side over the other and wrap it around me before tucking it into the skirt. I then take a thick black leather belt around my waist to cinch it and create a focal point and scrunch the sleeves up to my elbows. It looks polished and elevated, while also making me feel comfortable. Truly, the best of all worlds.

But now, it's time to finally get into your closet and get a sense of your own fashion sensibility. You may already have your power black dress or be one signature piece away from completing your most elevated yet comfortable look.

STEP 1: REVIEW THE ARCHIVES.

Do you have a picture of an outfit that you absolutely loved wearing? Write down the story of that outfit. How did you come to own each piece in that outfit? Do you remember what other looks you tried on before you settled on this one? What made this one click? What was the event you wore it to? What do you remember most about that night? How were the clothes a part of that memory?

Take note of a few key words from your answers. You will start to notice some repeating themselves as you do this for different looks, and your own unique style preferences will begin to reveal themselves.

If you start to see words like "feminine," "flirty," and "like a princess" then that's speaking to the story you want to tell. On the other hand, you may find yourself responding to outfits that make you feel "cool," "edgy," or "like a badass." There are no right or wrong answers. There's only what makes you feel your best and most confident self, and that's what we're out to find.

There may be a word that, in theory, you love, but in actuality, it's not practical and it's stressing you out. Words like "loud" and "outspoken" sound nice, but when you begin to think about it some more, you may find that's too aggressive for you. If it's providing stress, cut and run! If anything feels restrictive, we haven't unlocked the right words. Maybe where others are loud and outspoken you are distinct and memorable—you don't have to raise your voice to leave an impression. There shouldn't be an ounce of stress attached to these words. This should feel exactly like you. There might be some outliers too, words that are only connected to one example and found nowhere else in your list. That's OK. This might be an aspirational quality you want to integrate over time, or a little sprinkle you might add here and there.

What we are unlocking are the core elements that are integral to your authentic self. They should act as an anchor while also providing tremendous freedom.

STEP 2: STUDY YOUR REACTION.
Once we have a clear understanding of these foundations, we can turn to crafting our vision for the future. Now that you have a sense of your tastes and aesthetics, what happens when you take those clothes off the rack and throw them on your body? How do you react to wearing a certain color? What dress makes you throw back your shoulders and lift your chin, and which one has you constantly tugging on the hemline and crossing your legs?

First start by going into your own closet. This is an exercise I do with my clients. Try on everything you own—yes, I truly mean everything. How do you respond to each piece? Is there something in the back that you bought once but never wore because it looks too short or too long on the hanger? Put it on! No seriously, put it on right now. I'll wait. Do you remember why you bought it now? How does it make you feel? Why haven't you been wearing it? Should you change that?

Now go to a department store. This may take several hours to do, but pick a day and just go. Once you're there, try on everything. Yes, try it all on. First go through the things you love and gravitate toward. Ask yourself why: Is it because

> Your own personal style is yours alone. Don't let somebody else steer you wrong.

you truly feel good in it, or is it because someone once told you "This is for your body type"? Throw out every rule you've heard and see what you respond to.

Now go back to those racks. Try on the stuff you avoided. Question your gut assumption: What exactly do I hate about it? Is it the way it fits my body? Is it the color against my skin? Do you actually like it, even though you thought you would hate it? The answers may surprise you.

Remember, your own personal style is yours alone. Don't let somebody else steer you wrong.

STEP 3: FIND YOUR OWN "BLACK DRESS."

It's time to find your staple, the hero piece (or pieces) of your wardrobe. After you do all of this research about who you are and what you actually like, it's important to find your own personal classic item—like me and my Nike skirt. It might be a shockingly simple piece like an actual little black dress, or an oversized white button-down. It's something you know you feel comfortable in and look good in. It's probably a piece you find yourself reaching for or coming back to when you don't want to think about what you're putting on.

These pieces are invaluable. When you have so much going on in your life and there's all of this outside noise, it can be endlessly beneficial to have a go-to piece you know you never have to second guess or reconsider. If you can, buy a few of them so they are always at the ready (especially if it's versatile). You'll thank yourself later.

STEP 4: NOW ADD A POWER PIECE.

While your "black dress" is just a piece that you feel comfortable in and is likely versatile enough to be worn frequently, your power piece is something that sparks big emotions in you. For me, when I'm in something long that touches the floor, I feel empowered. There's something elegant and regal about the length that makes me stand taller. Even my walk changes. If you pay attention, you'll often see me in those pieces when I am on the red carpet or on a stage. These are my power pieces.

Maybe yours is something that's tight to your body or belted to show off your waist. Maybe it's just a fabulous blue shirt that shows off your décolletage (or any other enviable feature). If you're into one-of-a-kinds, look at pieces you've inherited or that were given to you: your mother's old necklace, your father's ring. There's even a chance it's the same as your "black dress" piece. Whatever it is, find those specific garments that you can lean on when you need a boost in your confidence. Scour high and low for the silhouette that you can put on when you wake up and you don't feel your best, so the process of putting it on will immediately elevate your mood and remind you of who you are. Trust me: your mood is what truly matters at the end of the day. When you feel good, you'll undeniably look good.

So go into your closet and start pulling together a new look. No, I mean it: Put it on now. Try a piece you haven't worn in a while that you've rediscovered that made you feel good. Now try adding in a power piece. If you don't feel a little brighter than before, that means we just need to keep searching until you find the right combination. Get to it!

IT'S DEEPER THAN YOU THINK

So many people ask me why I approach styling the way that I do; why do I focus on more than the clothes? How do I hone in on my client's individual needs and wants to create a look—a story, really—that transforms them on such a profound level? It hasn't been an overnight success—part of it comes from my academic background.

When I got to college, I didn't know what I wanted to study. I didn't want to be a doctor. I didn't want to be a teacher. I didn't want to be an engineer. I looked at myself and asked, *What else is left?* I decided that I would go into psychology.

After graduating, I spent two years working at a mental health organization doing intake work for new patients. My job required me to listen to countless stories of abuse and trauma—stories that made me ill. I would get physically sick from the gut-wrenching stories, and often they would keep me up at night. I didn't learn until later that I'm an empath, which meant that people's emotions affected me more intensely than most.

Those experiences are probably where my whole philosophy comes from. I spent hours upon hours sitting in a room with someone else, listening to their stories and watching their body language. I would try to pick up on certain clues through what they said, but also *how* they said it and what their body language communicated. Those are the exact skills and the instincts that I now use as a stylist: I watch and listen. *I can tell when to push someone out of their comfort zone, when to be more forceful with my vision, and when to pull back.* That's the psychologist's training.

My job is to bring out the desired aesthetic of whoever I'm dressing and to present the most elevated version of that. Even if I'm starting from scratch with someone, they already have something special in them, and it's my job to research and observe for added depth so that we can show that bit of magic in its most heightened state.

Sometimes I work with clients to totally revamp the story they're trying to tell, helping them craft a new, bolder, more authentic look. And sometimes I recognize the value in a client's story and current look and add to that by helping them refine it or ensuring that it evolves as they do.

The confidence to own your look is what sets icons apart. Whether you're admired for your distinctive sense of style, being a trendsetter, or being a classic beauty, if you own the story you're telling with your style, you're a bona fide fashion icon.

Years before she honored me at the CFDA Awards, Kerry Washington and I had one of our first fittings together. It was for a major red carpet: the 2020 Golden Globe awards.

In preparation, I did what I usually do, pulling racks of looks for her along with shoes and accessories and bringing it all to her home. I observed her reaction to the pieces as I asked her to identify what she loved and what she hated. Then I just watched as she separated them all. This process is so important: just like I told you to do, I studied her reaction to learn more about what was going on in her head when she first saw something.

There was one outfit—a dramatic ensemble from Altuzarra—that stopped her in her tracks. She seemed put off by it on the surface, but I looked deeper. I sensed it made her nervous and uncomfortable. That made sense: the look was basically an open blazer and a skirt. There was no top to it. However, I didn't see a full-throated refusal, which meant there was a chance. What I saw in Kerry's hesitation was an opportunity to help move her out of her comfort zone. I could tell that there was a little voice of fear in her head, and I was there to provide her with reinforcements for her voice of confidence.

This look was perfect for her. The long black satin skirt featured a thigh-high slit. The finishing touch was this incredible diamond belly chain. We kept the rest of the accessories and hair simple. The ensemble was distinctive and a showstopper. And ultimately, she was going to look beautiful no matter what.

When Kerry began working with me, we had a conversation about approaching her fashion and style in a different

> Watching her find the courage to try something out of her comfort zone, I was reminded just why I do what I do.

way than she was used to. We decided we were going to be a little more daring. The looks were going to be a little sexier. And they were going to make Kerry stand out on the carpet like the unique individual she is. To me, this elevated blazer and skirt look was the perfect follow-through on that intention. The effect was electric, and the response was overwhelming.

"Her style at past appearances on the Golden Globes red carpet has been described as being elegant and classic," *Harper's Bazaar* wrote about the look. "But this time around, she eschewed a safe silhouette for an outfit that was sultry and—with presumably the help of double-side tape—defied physics . . .

"So often, the blazer-and-skirt combo is the hallmark for proper office attire," they continued. "But with a bold chain in place of a blouse, and with the addition of a bold red lip, Washington gave a whole new meaning to the phrase *risky business*. And we're totally digging the updated definition." It ushered in our new era together. Watching her find the courage to try something out of her comfort zone, I was reminded just why I do what I do.

"Happiness comes from being who you actually are instead of who you think you are supposed to be."

—SHONDA RHIMES, *YEAR OF YES: HOW TO DANCE IT OUT, STAND IN THE SUN AND BE YOUR OWN PERSON*

04.

DON'T BE AFRAID
TO BE UNIQUE

Back in 2017, I accompanied the incomparable Ariana Grande on one of her trips to Japan. I remember it vividly.

We all know Ariana's look; it's iconic in that way. She often wears a short A-line skirt and a very tight, high ponytail. This isn't because she has to: Ariana is beautiful in any silhouette and gorgeous with any hairstyle. This was just what she chose as her signature look, and it was a silhouette that you can see in almost any context and instantly associate it with her. She faced criticism for keeping this style for so long, like so many successful, wildly talented, and famous young women do. I thought it was so perfect. Whatever your opinions on it as a style, you have to acknowledge it worked from a branding perspective.

I'll never forget the sight of hundreds of her fans waiting for her at the airport on that trip to Asia—all with high ponytails. What a compliment! Later, when she asked me how she should wear her hair on tour, I didn't hesitate. I think many stylists would want to put their stamp on a client. They'd want to be the ones who broke Ariana out of her "rut." But not me. I told her that if I was a fan and I bought a ticket to her show, and she *didn't* have a high ponytail, I would be devastated. I just knew that fans wanted that signature look. As long as it still made her feel good, there was no need to change it just because someone else said so.

My job was not to disrupt what Ariana was doing, but just to elevate it. I took on the challenge of creating growth and maturity while working within the paradigm of her look. Ariana is smart—she did not want to outgrow her audience. She taught me a valuable lesson in that, actually: when you hone into your own personal style and your strong sense of self, society shouldn't have a say in what will make you happy. I took it as my job, in part, to protect her in that way. To lean into her uniqueness.

When she first started with red carpets and appearances, Ariana was very young. She made her debut at sixteen on the Nickelodeon show *Victorious*. Her style at the time reflected her youth and inexperience—the color and fabric choices, the styles and how she put together an outfit. As she was growing up and the music matured, we decided to keep much of her look the same but do it in a new way. It was a little bit sexier. Instead of pink or pastels, she'd wear black vinyl. Or we'd pair the short skirt with the va va voom of over-the-knee boots. It was always her, but elevated and with a new, more mature perspective that comes with age.

It was my job to stay true to her brand and make her looks iconic. And over the span of her Dangerous Woman tour, thirteen music videos, and a Met Gala appearance, I think we did just that. The visuals became so on-brand that when Givenchy teased her as the face of their latest campaign in 2019, the whole world knew who it was just based on her silhouette alone.

That's what we should all be striving for—that sort of singularity. There's only one you. Each of us is unique, with our own special blend of experiences, talents, and perspectives. Being an icon is about leveraging that authenticity, which will only embolden your confidence. That's *your* superpower. You'll attract people and opportunities that genuinely align with your values and interests. You'll build meaningful, fulfilling relationships and make choices that lead to a more exciting and purpose-driven life.

In other words, individuality is about building a life you love. Be unapologetically you and watch those connections flourish.

NEVER ASK PERMISSION TO BE WHO YOU ARE

Have you ever seen someone walking down the street who just doesn't care what anyone else thinks? When I go to New York City, people watching is one of my favorite things, and this is my favorite type of person to watch. You know, the person wearing a polka dot shirt and striped pants with red shoes and blue bows in their hair. You can't imagine the thought process that went into putting that outfit together and leaving the house, but damn if they aren't feeling themselves. They are strutting down the sidewalk. In fact, while watching them you find yourself questioning your own assumption: maybe it isn't a bad look after all! The way you wear your clothes is just as important as, if not more important than, what you're wearing.

> The way you wear your clothes is just as important as, if not more important than, what you're wearing.

Style is a tool of expression, so I encourage you to be your truest self and not to seek approval or validation from others. You should never feel the need to conform to societal expectations, norms, or the opinions of others when it comes to your identity, beliefs, vision, and how you demonstrate that through your style.

This mindset promotes self-confidence, self-acceptance, and the courage to pursue your passions, dreams, and individuality without being hindered by fear or the desire for external approval. It's a reminder that your worth and identity are not determined by others but by your own sense of self and purpose. And that confidence will speak louder than any fashion rule that's been handed down to you over the years.

Ultimately, you must live your life on your own terms. When you're comfortable with who you are, you're more likely to have a positive self-image and be less affected by external judgments or the need for validation from others. This inner strength enables you to navigate through challenges more effectively.

In the age of social media, where everyone's life highlights are on display, it's easy to fall into the trap of comparing yourself to others. We all know that constant comparison can be detrimental to our mental and emotional well-being. But sometimes we can't help ourselves. It can be helpful in those moments to have a mantra or affirmation you say to yourself. You don't even have to be creative, you can borrow some Beyoncé lyrics: "I'm one of one. I'm number one. I'm the only one." This type of self-talk is important.

Do things your own way. Question everything. You are unique, with a one-of-a-kind vision, point of view, and skill set. Be the uncensored version of yourself. Don't try to imitate someone else's style; instead, focus on what makes you, you. Be like Mary J Blige.

I've grown up with Mary J Blige—we all have, really. But in 2017 I started working with her, which to be honest is a big deal to people who look like me. She is the Queen of Hip-Hop Soul and the blueprint for the style of quite a few Black women you know. She's the epitome of a certain type of Black glamour, so my job was finding ways of continually elevating that. Specifically, as I was brought on for her *Mudbound* press tour, envisioning what Mary J Blige the actress would look like on the red carpet was essential.

During our time together, Mary was turning up on the Met Gala red carpet and performing onstage at the Oscars, some of the most glamorous places in the world. But it was important to us to never lose who she was. She made that clear in our first fitting.

I had brought racks and racks of clothes out for her and was pitching her on my vision. I knew who she was and what she had looked like before—I had done my homework like I had done with every other client before her. But I thought it was time to try something new. As I explained to her, she was going to be on carpets next to all of these venerated actresses, so I brought her these sophisticated dresses and elegant suits. The vision was for her to be aligned with what was going on. She looked at my options and her reply was very simple. "I know what I like," she said. My response was equally simple. "Say no more," I told her as I steered her over to a rack that I had prepared with catsuits, furs, tall boots, and leather. She knew exactly who she was, and believe me, I did too. I had hoped to pitch her on what was a pretty drastic switch on her look, and she wasn't ready for that. I could tell instantly that it wasn't the time to push her, so I showed her the other options I had prepared—I never go anywhere without being prepared for anything.

The pieces on the second rack were the Mary we all know and love. Her looks were about being alive, sexy, classy, and ghetto fabulous all at the same time—those are Mary's own words. And we didn't change any of that for anyone's red carpet. At that point in her life, those attributes took on additional meaning: Mary was fresh out of a divorce, so being free and sexy was exactly how she felt. Over time I started to interject some new things, helping to elevate her aesthetic, but it was always about making sure she felt powerful in every single look. Making sure that we never lost her, no matter how elevated the look turned out to be.

W Magazine (and others) said Mary "stole the night" at the 2018 Met Gala, when we worked with Versace. The theme was "Heavenly Bodies," and Donatella made her an amazing draped blue gown with gold appliqué embroidered over the bodice and a high thigh slit that perfectly showed her figure. We completed the look with an MJB trademark: matching over-the-knee boots. "It's so Mary J Blige in a gown," Mary told *Vogue* about the look. "Everyone knows I love boots. So this could have never gone wrong. This was perfect." For me, it was the perfect blend of the two Marys, the music icon and the actress. It was

Me at age two *(Courtesy of the author)*

Grandma Carolyn with a close family friend *(Courtesy of the author)*

FROM TOP: Grandparents James Roach Sr. and Eloise Roach; (from left) grandfather James Roach Sr., James Roach Jr. ("Uncle Jimmy"), uncles Larry Roach, Rodney Roach, Aaron Roach (holding me), and the late Frank Roach; me as a young child (*Courtesy of the author*)

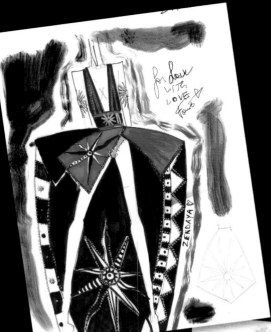

THIS PAGE, CLOCKWISE FROM TOP LEFT: Zendaya by Fausto Puglisi; the "Law" boot by Ruthie Davis for Ariana Grande; Zendaya by Fausto Puglisi *(All images courtesy of the designers);* OPPOSITE: Zendaya by Donatella Versace for Versace

ATELIER
VERSACE

Zendaya

With Z at the HBO Max FYC event for her show *Euphoria* in April 2022 *(Amy Sussman/Getty Images)*

TOP LEFT: The first look we did together, for the *Justin Bieber: Never Say Never* premiere at the Nokia Theatre in LA *(Jon Kopaloff/FilmMagic)*; TOP RIGHT: One of the most talked-about looks at the 2018 Met Gala's Heavenly Bodies theme was Z's ode to Joan of Arc in a custom Versace. *(Theo Wargo/Getty Images)*; BOTTOM: Z and I wear custom Tommy Hilfiger at the 2019 Met Gala red carpet. The theme was "Camp: Notes on Fashion." I was Z's fairy godmother, complete with a wand. *(Gotham/GC Images)*

Adjusting Zendaya's 1996 Givenchy gown by John Galliano at the 2024 Met Gala. The theme was "Sleeping Beauties: Reawakening Fashion." *(Taylor Hill/Getty Images)*

Me wearing Duckie Brown and Z wearing a Rick Owens gown at the *Dune* UK Special Screening in London in October 2021 *(Samir Hussein/WireImage)*

Accompanying Z to the *Dune: Part Two* world premiere in London, February 2024. I am wearing a coat by The Attico, and Z is wearing an archival cyborg suit from Thierry Mugler's Fall/Winter 1995 couture collection. *(Joe Maher/Getty Images)*

Behind the scenes with the one and only Céline Dion *(Denise Truscello)*

Backstage at the 66th Grammy Awards with Céline Dion. I am wearing LR3, and Céline is wearing Valentino Couture. *(Emma McIntyre/Getty Images for The Recording Academy)*

TOP: Megan Thee Stallion wearing custom Paco Rabanne and me wearing Willy Chavarria at the *Hollywood Reporter* and Jimmy Choo Power Stylists Dinner, March 28, 2023 *(Donato Sardella/ Getty Images)*; BOTTOM: I presented Z with the Style Star award at the third annual InStyle Awards in 2017. *(Matt Winkelmeyer/Getty Images)*

Kerry Washington and me, in custom Oscar de la Renta, behind the scenes at the CFDA Fashion Awards in 2022. It was an honor to have her present me with their first Stylist Award. *(Jason Mendez/Getty Images)*

Me in custom Valentino by Pier Paolo Piccioli at the TIME100 Next event in October 2022
(Craig Barritt/Getty Images)

one of a couple of stunning looks from that press tour (she wore an amazing off the shoulder custom white Vera Wang gown to perform at the Oscars, as all-white has long been one of her favorite looks). And all of those looks were unmistakably Mary.

Showing up as you are in every space tells the world something. It tells everyone watching that you know who you are. It's affirmation to yourself that who you are deserves to be in all of those spaces as well. Of course, there are certainly levels to it—a glamorous version of your signature look that is appropriate for a gala might be different than the version of you running to the corner store—but the essence of you should always be there. You will be more at home in any space if you feel comfortable in your own clothes.

DROWNING OUT APPREHENSION

Too often, people don't put themselves out there because of fear. Fear of change, fear of the unknown, and fear of discomfort can all cause you to feel stuck. The same is true after success. When you've accomplished something significant and reached a new level of performance in any area of your life, you may find yourself faced with fear yet again. Success can be as crippling as failure: the stakes are higher, and you're likely to be more visible and have more pressure on you. Often you'll wonder what's next now that you've accomplished what you set out to do and feel paralyzed about the "comedown" from the top. Fear too often prevents people from even trying. And this is something that just about anyone can experience.

Megan Thee Stallion is one of the most incredible rappers out there and happens to be a truly gorgeous woman on top of it. We first met in 2019 while filming a reality TV show together (more on that once-in-a-lifetime experience in the next chapter). We instantly connected and spent time together, showing up at the same events and staying in touch.

When she finally called me to work together in March 2022, it wasn't a "what took you so long," but more of a "now is the perfect time." (Although I had been waiting to get my hands on her for a while.) We did a little bit of everything together: performances, magazine covers, red carpets, we did it all. But then she took a step back from the public spotlight for about six months in light of some personal issues that became front-page news. When she was ready to come back, she called me to help shape her reintroduction to the world.

The moment was the 2023 *Vanity Fair* Oscar Party. We knew it had to be special. Megan had just lost some weight and had this new update on her already breathtaking figure to show off. She was feeling really good about herself and where she was in her life, and she wanted to make sure people knew it.

I was excited to see Meg again as I went to fit her for the event; it had been a few months since we'd seen each other. When I walked in, she was in workout clothes with no makeup and wearing her natural hair. Normally, she's in full glam: wigs, full makeup, the whole thing. It's standard for female rappers today: the longest, most luxurious wigs and glam done to perfection have become the norm. When I saw her with no makeup and natural hair, I was mesmerized by her beauty. And a lightbulb went off.

"You're glowing. You look beautiful," I told her. And with a wink, I suggested, "You've never been on a carpet like this." Sure, fans might have seen it on social media, but never with the full glam of a red-carpet moment.

She quickly shot me down. We went back and forth, but I didn't push her. Whatever the look ended up being, it had to be on her terms. (But I knew she could pull it off.)

The dress we chose was dramatic. She wore a custom Bach Mai strapless mermaid gown with a netted, corseted bust. It was fitted and hugged her curves. The jewelry was classic and glamorous, including a diamond choker necklace and diamond chandelier earrings.

The next day, I texted her to tell her I'd had a dream about her wearing her natural hair. That's how it happens for me sometimes: I dream about someone, or some big decision or moment. But it feels more like a vision. I feel such a visceral, soulful calling toward a certain look, a dress, a moment, or a decision in my life, that in some cases I can't help but share it. It's definitely not a mandate my clients are forced to follow. Think of it more as a gentle wink.

Thankfully, Meg trusted me. She felt my sincere love for her and my heartfelt desire to create a moment on the red carpet that would be absolutely magical. She agreed to wear her natural hair.

The day of the event, though, she had second thoughts. She texted me, "Law, I don't know about this hair. What do you think about this other hairstyle?" Her fear was that the dress was too polished to have her hair out—she thought the freeness of her hair would clash and even cover up her neck and shoulders. Her nervousness to be back out on the scene in general was making it worse. It was clear to me she just needed a little reassurance. Stepping on the red carpet with your natural hair as a woman in an industry where that's not the norm can feel a little vulnerable. But Meg was stunning, and being her authentic self in this moment was going to make the biggest statement of all.

I told her: "Megan, there's no other hairstyle. I've seen it. Please, baby, just trust me." I decided I needed to go to her, so I arrived at her hotel suite where she was getting ready. I walked into the room, kissed her on the cheek, and looked at her in the mirror. Her hair was gorgeous, curled, free, and long, flowing past her shoulders. She slipped on the dress, and I could tell she was feeling it. "You look beautiful. You look perfect." I do not bullshit anyone: I could see the power and the energy that radiated from this gorgeous woman, and I reflected it back to her, strengthening her existing confidence.

On the red carpet, you could tell she was alive in her skin. She was touching her hair, pushing it up or off her face, leaning into the drama of her new look. The movement and the whole romantic vibe of the dress, the silhouette, the jewelry, the glam—it all came together.

The next day, she said, "Thank you for pushing me out of my comfort zone." And I thanked her for trusting me. That moment of her, which went viral online, would have never happened if Megan wasn't confident enough to drown out her apprehension and negative thoughts. I was there to help her, but ultimately it all fell on her when she hit that carpet. No one else would have made that happen. The consensus was that she'd never looked better. *Harper's Bazaar* called it a "grand return"; *W* described it as "regal"; *Vogue* trumpeted it as "glorious." She was back!

It's important to remember that fear will not kill you.

It's important to remember that fear will not kill you. Staying stuck, meanwhile, *will* dim your light and prevent you from finding out what you're capable of. You'll leave whole parts of yourself unexplored for no reason. Because here's the thing: we're all going to make mistakes. I've seen myself on the red carpet the morning after an event and wished I could have changed things. In 2021 I walked the red carpet at the Met Gala in a silhouette that was mostly familiar to me but with hair that was . . . let's just say "a little different."

I decided to go with nice full dreadlocks that came to about chin length. Would I have done some things differently if I had more time to focus on myself and my look? Probably. But I don't mind seeing the images. I don't necessarily regret them. That night was about living in that moment. I felt cool. Instead of worrying about what commenters might say later, I went on those steps feeling really blessed to be there. Photographers not only knew who I was but wanted to take my picture. Those were wins in my book.

I acknowledge that it's not all good. But I know that I will learn from every experience. I don't beat myself up. I'm willing to take risks. Resilience is trying, failing, building on those misses, and trying again, and again, and again. Failure and success go hand in hand. Any moment where I feel that I might not have hit the mark perfectly, I don't put much energy into it because I always know there will be another moment. I know that I am more than one instance. You are too.

It's not about the first miss, or the messy second try. It's about the fourth, the fifth, or the hundredth time that you go for it and prove to yourself that you can do it. It doesn't matter if it hurts, or if it looks ugly. It matters that you get up and go back and try again. Resilience is built through action. A resilient person views pressure as privilege, setbacks as temporary, and obstacles as opportunity. And believe me, you'll never regret saying "yes" to yourself one more time.

There is a lot of noise out there telling women how to be: lean in, lean out, be feminine, be strong, become a #GirlBoss or a #BossBitch (but also be kind and gentle and take care of yourself), meditate, journal, and buy this lipstick! It's enough to make your head spin! In the age of constant connection and never-ending demands of our time and energy, the world expects us to be superhumans who can conquer the world and hang on even when the going gets tough. Don't listen to "experts" and these so-called rules. Remember, you create the rules of what works for you.

Our concern about what others think about us can be a significant barrier to reaching our full potential. When we are overly preoccupied

TAKE ACTION: LEARN TO LET GO OF FEAR

Everyone has fears, and it's likely that many of us have shied away from standing out. I moved around a lot growing up, meaning there were a lot of first days of school in front of new classes. I came to dread them.

Kids can be mean, and growing up with a name like Law Roach definitely doesn't make that easier. I came to hate my name in those earlier years because it made me stand out in ways I did not like. Some of the other students would come up with derogatory nicknames for me. But with time, that began to change. That distinctive, unique quality became a double-edged sword in that my name was surely unforgettable. It's the center of my brand now and something I would never think of changing.

The tricky thing about confidence is just because you're confident doesn't mean fear does not exist. There might always be that little voice of fear in your head. The point is to give it no power—to let it go, as it does not serve you. You want to make the voice of confidence overpower that fear and allow you to accomplish things that fear made you think were unimaginable. Once you learn how to navigate it when it rears its ugly head, then you will truly be unstoppable and able to overcome anything that stands in the way of your pursuit of success.

Here's your ultimate guide on how to let go of that fear of failure, or change, or transformation, or whatever is holding you back. It's been a good reminder time and time again that fear does not hold power over me.

- **Acknowledge Your Fear.** First, let's call out that fear—give it a name and tell it to fuck off. Be honest with yourself about what you're afraid of and *why*. Acknowledging it is the first step to taking control.

- **Understand Your Fear.** Try to understand the source of your fear. Is it based on past experiences, irrational beliefs, or external pressures? Understanding the root cause can help you confront it.

- **Repeat Positive Affirmations.** Swap those negative thoughts for positive affirmations. When fear whispers, "You can't do it," shout back, "I CAN and I WILL!"

- **Seek Community Support.** Reach out to your friends, family, or an online community. Sharing your fears can be liberating, and getting support from your tribe is like a warm, comforting hug. My clients like Megan can call or text me at a moment's notice when they need some support. Is there a person or group of people you can lean on in times of hardship?

- **Educate Yourself.** Knowledge is power. The more you know about what you fear, the more you can handle it. Dig deep and empower yourself with information.

- **Stay Present.** Fear often lives in the future, because the future is the only thing that's truly unknowable. Enjoy the way you feel right now. Bask in that experience. Stop considering what someone might think or say about you later. Stay in the now because you've got this moment locked down!

- **Challenge Yourself.** Push those boundaries! The more you challenge fear, the weaker it becomes. Even though I have some tried and true hairstyles I know will work for me, I'm always experimenting with something new. Every time I do, I feel a bit freer to try something else.

- **Be Kind to Yourself.** It's OK to be afraid. But be kind to yourself because you're your own biggest cheerleader.

- **Stay Persistent.** Keep pushing, keep fighting, and never back down. You are a warrior, and fear is no match for your determination!

- **Realize "Failure" Is a Matter of Perspective.** I often say that what seems like failure is the universe's protection or direction. If something doesn't go as you thought, you not only get a better handle on what you should be doing, but maybe you'll learn something about yourself or those around you in the process. Every single step is an opportunity for growth.

with seeking approval or avoiding criticism, we may hold ourselves back from taking risks, expressing our true selves, and pursuing our goals with confidence. This fear of judgment can create self-doubt, anxiety, and a reluctance to step outside our comfort zones.

When I first moved to Los Angeles, I will admit, I had some fears. I was moving to a new place where I didn't really know a whole lot of people. I was also trying to break into an industry where I didn't have many connections. If I didn't feel different in those early days, I certainly looked it. The other stylists at the time were mostly white and mostly women. And so I tried to change myself to fit in. I never doubted my own talent, but I had a fear that people wouldn't accept me enough to even see my skills.

It might sound silly now, but I changed the way I talked. I tried to adopt a sort of Valley girl way of speaking. I thought that if I sounded like everyone else, maybe I would fit in more. Maybe I would be accepted and that then I could show everyone what I was capable of. It was exhausting. Trying to police who you are is a full-time job, and it just wasn't for me. But I quickly found that it was in the moments where my unique and authentic personality came out that I made real connections.

The experience that solidified that notion came with Céline Dion. As we began to see each other more, as we worked together and I began letting my guard down, she continued to treat me with the same respect that I saw her treat everyone else with. In fact, I saw her go further. In one of our first photoshoots, there was a moment when I wasn't being heard by the rest of the creative team as I gave feedback on direction. They wanted to do something that I just knew would not work for Céline. It was frustrating, and I felt like I was being ignored by everyone. But I wasn't.

Céline pulled me to the side and said something that has stuck with me since then: "You are special and you are incredible. If anybody ever treats you less than what you deserve, you tell me." To have this global superstar see me as special and incredible was validating, especially because she knew so much about me and the way that I talked and where I came from. If she could see it, then anyone could. That's how I felt. So I cast aside that fear and leaned into being me in all of that specialness.

Getting over my initial fear not only brought me much less stress, but also led to the success that I have today. You might not have a Céline speaking to you face-to-face, but I want to tell you: you are special. Each one of us is. You deserve to live in that specialness, to explore it and show it to the world. And for most of us, one of the biggest obstacles hindering us is fear. Are you going to continue to let it stop you?

I want to tell you: you are special. Each one of us is.

STOP YOUR INTERNAL COMPARISON

When you let go of the comparison game, you'll realize that everyone else has their own identity, so there really is no point in comparing. You will start to celebrate what makes you different rather than strive to fit in. You will learn that good style is a myth, and that the only thing that truly exists is personal style. And remember, you can't please everyone. Instead of worrying about what other people think, focus on what you have to say.

Constantly comparing oneself to others, especially on social media where you have no context, can lead to feelings of inadequacy or inferiority. The pressure to meet these false standards set by others can be overwhelming, causing unnecessary stress. Embracing your individuality and unique qualities is truly the best antidote for comparison. You're already on your own path, doing your own thing. Focus on your own goals and self-discovery so that there is no time to worry about what anyone else is doing.

For me, because of my own gateway into fashion, it could have been easy to compare myself to every other stylist. I could have wallowed in not having connections with major fashion houses. I could have complained about people telling us no because I represented a lot of Black girls or women who weren't sample size. But instead, I embraced it all and used it to push my success.

If big names weren't going to lend clothes to me, I had no problem in sourcing exciting young designers to put on my clients. It's the same thing I did at Deliciously Vintage—if it was a show-stopping look, who cared who the designer was? And better yet, it was an opportunity to share our platform with a community of creatives and help boost their businesses. Before we knew it, everyone wanted to know about this new, young designer who made these looks.

I also found myself going back to my vintage roots. I say this as humbly as possible, but no working stylist was putting vintage garments on the red carpet like I was. No one. I've been putting my clients in vintage since the very beginning of my career, a lot of it out of my own personal archive. In an industry that's constantly talking about how to be more sustainable, this seemed to me to be the ultimate in sustainability.

In 2022, I did some work with the global supermodel Bella Hadid—I think she actually came to me because she saw my talents pulling from the archives. Most of what I put her in for and around Cannes that year was vintage: a 1959 dress by Yves Saint Laurent for Christian Dior; a black gown from Gianni Versace's Spring 1987 collection; a gorgeous, slinky gown from Donatella's Fall 2001 Versace collection for a Chopard event; as well as a fun black-and-white look from Karl Lagerfeld's Fall 1986 Chanel collection. While it's more common to see young designers or vintage looks on the red carpet these days, I started doing it because those were my own personal skills. This is what made me an individual and unique from other stylists at the time.

Life unfolds at a different pace for everyone. Your experiences, opportunities, and challenges are distinct from those of your peers. While someone may seem to have it all together or be on a different path, you just never know the circumstances of their life. The accomplishments you achieve in your twenties do not necessarily determine your future success or happiness. People often reach significant milestones at various times in their lives. Comparing your progress to others can create not only unnecessary pressure and impatience but stifle personal growth, harm emotional well-being, and hinder the pursuit of one's authentic self.

Embracing the uniqueness of your journey, understanding the unpredictable nature of timelines, and fostering positive relationships are all compelling reasons to resist the urge to compare yourself to others. Any moment can be a period of self-discovery, growth, and fulfillment. Take a step back, focus on your individual path, and appreciate the beauty of your unique journey without constantly measuring it against others. Trust me, it's worth it.

ENERGY AND INTENTION

Every day you will be battered with distractions. Especially with the Internet and social media; there's a lot of noise out there. It's important to keep your purpose front and center at all times. You will need it. There will be moments, big and small, when you have choices to make, and you owe it to yourself to give those choices the attention they need.

While I thrive on multitasking, when I'm with a client, I try to center all my energy and intention around them. As I began to step in front of the cameras from behind the clothing racks, that became more complicated. In the early days of working with Céline Dion, I was also just starting with my first season of *America's Next Top Model* (I was a judge on cycles 23 and 24). One day when I was escorting Céline to an event, there was a group of girls yelling for our attention. The assumption was universal: they were there for the global star we all grew up with. But it became clear to us that they weren't. They had seen me on *ANTM* and wanted a photo with me.

I was confused if I'm being honest. I told them I would take Céline inside to her event and then come back out to meet them. But it was something I thought about for a while after, trying to figure out how to balance both sides of my work. This was the real birth of my Sasha Fierce wig: my thought process was that when crowds saw me in this long, bone-straight hair, they would know that I was the star. They could come up to me and take pictures and introduce themselves. But if I had any other hairstyle, I was meant to blend into the background, not to be noticed. This was by my design.

It didn't work as intended, as the public didn't pick up on the hint. But I do think it worked for my mental state and energy, to compartmentalize in this way. It helped me get in the right mindset for my focus in what was becoming an increasingly hectic life. That physical change had a mental impact on me that really helped in the early days.

Intentionality empowers effective decision-making. When individuals are aware of their goals and values, they can make choices that are in alignment with their overarching objectives. Whether it is a choice in the workplace, personal life, or education, intentionality guides us toward decisions that are most beneficial for us, reducing the likelihood of regrets or missteps.

Knowing the why behind our efforts can bolster resilience during challenging times. When you face obstacles or setbacks, your clear
intentions can help you stay motivated and focused as you overcome them.

When we get busy, distracted, frustrated, or overwhelmed, we
rarely pause to reorient ourselves. But you need to reflect, to check in
with yourself to make sure wherever you're heading is taking you to
where—and who—you want to be.

Start by considering these questions:

- What am I chasing? And why?

- With all of this demand on me day in and day out, what is
  being compromised? Am I OK with that?

- Do my values align with where I put my energy?

  Or, the bigger questions, like:

- What do I want my legacy to be?

- How do I want people to describe me?

You can be intentional in all areas of your life. That may look like
prioritizing one activity or goal above the others. When you concen-
trate on one task, you can allocate your mental resources more effectively, maintain a higher level of concentration, and complete that
task more efficiently. It can also reduce stress and help you feel a
sense of accomplishment as you complete each task no matter how
big or small.

Ultimately, that was the lesson Godmother Eunice was trying to teach me when she asked me why I was still living in Chicago. If it was my intention to be a top Hollywood stylist, would I be able to do that where I was? I've trusted in myself to take that intention and see it through all the way.

If you feel stuck, ask yourself, what are your intentions? Are your actions aligning with them? If not, this might be the time to make a big move.

"You can't let anyone tell
you what your best is. You know
what your best is."

—BEYONCÉ,
ON *PIERS MORGAN LIVE*

05.

ALWAYS STAY INSPIRED

When I first moved to New York City years ago—this was when everyone referred to Bushwick as Bushwick and not East Williamsburg—I met my friend Nick. At the time, we were two young gay Black boys living in New York City and obsessed with all things fashion, beauty, and glamour. We both ended up working in fashion—he now works at a luxury brand. But back then it was clear to me that Nick knew at least a little bit more than I did, so whenever I would go over to his house, I would find myself asking questions.

Nick was one of those people who would tear pages out of magazines, buy posters, and more to tack to his walls. This was before social media like we know it today, but he surrounded himself with these images of Black glamour and Black beauty. He was obsessed with it. Photographs of the legendary model Naomi Sims were right beside images of the actress Jayne Kennedy. All the greats, some I had never heard of, were there. So I would ask about who these women were, and when I got home I would look them up. I did the same thing when I was home watching the news or old movies with my grandfather. Who was this woman or that woman? And then I would find a way to read their stories.

I still do this today, you know. I'm constantly watching movies and old documentaries—*Mahogany* with Diana Ross is one of my favorites. I'm also always falling down rabbit holes on Instagram or TikTok while in the car on the way to my next appointment or waiting for a food order alone. There's a constant stream of inspiration and education from so many sources at the touch of our fingers, and if you pay attention to my work, you'll see evidence of these inspirations everywhere: doing an ode or an homage to an old movie or even buying an actual piece of history and putting it on a client (or myself) to revitalize it. It was something amazing to put into practice in a major way back in 2019.

I was blessed enough to be asked by Zendaya to serve as a creative director for a set of collections she did with Tommy Hilfiger that year. For the project we decided to do two major shows: one in Harlem and one in Paris. The second show was inspired by the 1973 Battle of Versailles, a historic fashion show that many say earned American designers respect on the international stage.

The Battle of Versailles was a fundraiser intended to raise money for the restoration of the Palace of Versailles. The show put US-based brands like Oscar de la Renta and Halston in a fight with French brands like Yves Saint Laurent and Christian Dior. The American brands won, and it was largely due to the amazing runway performances of the mostly Black models they had cast, who displayed what *Women's Wear Daily* called "a more liberated view of femininity." The moment became a landmark in fashion history and demand for casting Black American models spiked afterward. For our Paris show, Zendaya and I decided to honor their contributions.

Going backstage at that show was really like watching my inspiration feed come to life. Every model in the show was Black. And more than that, we didn't just cast the current expected names like Jourdan Dunn and Winnie Harlow; we went back to the OG models. Pat Cleveland, who walked in the original show, was there, as was Beverly Johnson, Veronica Webb, Beverly Peele, Debra Shaw, Chrystele Saint Louis Augustin, and Brandi Quinones. These were the women who not only inspired Zendaya and me but paved the way to make it even possible to do what we do.

I kept getting chills throughout the process from being in the same space with so many of these inspirational women. To not only have the opportunity to be in the room with all of them—and ask questions I've always been curious about—but also help educate the next generation about our history gave me goosebumps. That is really the whole point of the work that I do. But it was only possible, and we were only able to put that sort of intention into the show, because of these bits of history and culture we've collectively picked up along the way.

This process of finding inspiration in history and those that came before had made us more confident in who we were and what we were doing, which ultimately gave us the platform to do something that's always been important to us both: to give back. Inspiration is often the fuel that keeps your creative engine (and mood) high. It can turn an everyday outfit into a conversation starter because you've sourced inspiration from your favorite piece of art. Or it can turn a fashion show meant to sell clothes into a teaching moment for the world.

> # Inspiration is often the fuel that keeps your creative engine (and mood) high.

HOW TO BE LEGENDARY

One of the craziest experiences of my life was sitting in the judges' chair on the HBO competition show *Legendary*. It's a show that celebrates ballroom culture, a movement led by queer and trans creators of color known for its unique blend of dance, fashion, and self-expression. It's had a massive impact on pop culture—a lot of popular language today comes from the scene, as well as voguing. *Legendary* featured ten houses each season, each consisting of performers who compete in different categories of ballroom like face, performance (voguing), and runway. The goal was to impress the judges—which included my girl Megan Thee Stallion, Jameela Jamil, Leiomy Maldonado, Keke Palmer, and myself at different points throughout the three seasons—and win the title of Legendary House.

I've had so many friends who have been part of ballroom over the years. I always supported them and attended balls, though I never personally had the courage to walk a category. But I enjoyed the artistry and family-like camaraderie in the scene. I often tell this story about going to a ball in the early 2000s. I was already interested in fashion at the time, but that night blew my mind.

Ballroom has many categories that people compete in, but some of my favorites are obviously the fashion categories. There are categories for streetwear or accessories and also for high-fashion garments. The point of it all is to pull off the most sickening look, with exclusive pieces that make peoples' jaws drop. I remember seeing Thaddeus, who was then in the House of Mizrahi, hit the back of the runway one night. He was wearing this ruffled Christian Lacroix satin blazer, heels, and panties from Gucci's Tom Ford era with the metallic GG on them. My mind was blown. I thought he was so beautiful in a way I didn't know men were allowed to be at the time. This was before it was more common to be gender nonconforming or to dress in genderless ways. I really hadn't ever seen a man dress like that and be applauded for it.

If you ever have been to a ball or even seen a clip, you know how overwhelming that applause can be. People chanting your house name, stomping on the ground and clapping. I distinctly remember his confidence and the way he held himself. It's a moment I'll never stop talking about, and what I witnessed that night helped shape the person I am today.

The confidence Thaddeus had is truly at the heart of ballroom. If you watch *Paris Is Burning*, you hear Junior LaBeija talking about having the "nerve to walk a ballroom floor." Nerve is just confidence by another name. It takes so much belief to put yourself out there as the center of attention in front of all of your peers and say "Not only do I deserve to be here, but I'm better than these other people." That's really what you have to believe when you hit the back of the runway of a ball.

Another category I love is face, which is really the living embodiment of confidence. Sure, on the surface face is about bone structure, perfect skin, and flawless teeth, but when competitors hit the floor, it's about selling it. It's about oozing all the self-confidence you have inside, outwardly in a way that can bring a whole room to its feet without a word. That "sellage," that's the power of true charisma. Some people call it emoting, but it's like you can feel the confidence pouring out of the best face divas. It's in Leyna Miyake Mugler's smoldering eyes or the way she runs her finger along her nose. Or with Lola Gucci, it's in her stare: just standing there, immovable but defiant at the House of Lanvin's Ball in 2023. It's confidence that got an entire room clapping and stomping their feet. And of course, it won Lola $10,000 that night.

When people decide to walk a ball, they know that every single one of their competitors is going to be drop dead gorgeous. Every single person will be flawless. But they hold on to one thing that takes them over, consumes them throughout the competition: *She's not me.* That is a type of confidence that defies all odds.

When actress Jameela Jamil called me about doing *Legendary*, I said yes immediately. She was already signed on as a judge, and I credit her creative vision with bringing together the personalities that made the show what it was. I was drawn to using my platform to expose people to the incredible qualities of the ballroom community that I had cherished for so long.

I think that ballroom is one of the last subcultures to really get its moment in the spotlight. It's the epitome of the kind of storytelling, boldness, innovation, and risk-taking that inspires me to my core. Each ball has a theme, and competitors work with their houses to make their visions come to life. Their chosen siblings and parents function as stylists, creative directors, and choreographers to pull off these truly inspiring moments.

I crafted a persona for the show. Though I had already done *America's Next Top Model*, *Legendary* was different. It required me to push the envelope even further. Since ballroom is a land of exaggeration and fantasy, I put that into the character I created. I pushed it to the point of almost-delusional confidence. I used some of who I am and amped it up even more. I was always known as the one who was quick-witted and super honest, even if that sometimes came off as mean. Simon Cowell was my inspiration in some ways—love him or hate him, you're still talking about him.

And as for my looks, I also pushed the envelope there as well. A central part of ballroom is the power of taking risks and putting yourself out there. For three seasons and countless hours, I saw incredible people commit to their performances, to their teammates, and to their bold, over-the-top looks. So I did the same, going full-throttle on weekly themes, completely switching my look every episode. I took all the things I knew about the scene, the language, the way face competitors run their tongues over their pearly white teeth, and their rock-solid self-assurance and turned it all into this character who was ultimately just Law Roach on steroids.

When I look back on it, I can see that skill I learned from my mother many years ago. I had been watching competition shows for so long that I knew what worked and what fell short. The character that I had created was perfect for the job I was doing, which was to make good television. The audience (for the most part) loved it, and I enjoyed showing this side of myself that felt right at home in ballroom.

NEVER STOP TAKING RISKS

Progression is all about shaking up the status quo, breaking the mold, and thinking way outside the box. Who wants to blend in when you can stand out?

Now, when we talk about innovation, it's not just about creating the next fabulous fashion trend—although that's definitely a part of it! It's about pushing boundaries, rewriting the rules, and shaking up the world in your very own life. Who wants to be boring when you can be groundbreaking? You can explore uncharted territories in style, create fashion statements that turn heads, and let your inner creativity run wild. We are each the designers of our own destiny!

Taking risks is essential for self-discovery, creativity, and making a lasting impression. As you can tell by now, I have quite a track record of encouraging my clients to step out of their comfort zones and experiment with unconventional combinations, bold colors, unique silhouettes, and unexpected accessories. The most memorable and impactful fashion moments come from taking daring chances. Whether it's on the red carpet or in everyday life, enjoy the freedom that comes with trying something new and unconventional.

The most memorable and impactful fashion moments come from taking daring chances.

This is something I also do myself. I'm always trying out a new look or piece. I do it the most with my hair, which isn't really common for a man. Wearing my Sasha Fierce wig with my perfectly groomed facial hair isn't conventional. Neither are any of my other wig styles. It's a risk every day to stick to my style, especially in front of new audiences. You never know what the response may be. But this is me, and I will not change myself for anyone.

I'm not the first person, by far, to look like this though. To be truthful, I remember the person who inspired me. It was Andre J.!

When I was in New York in the early 2000s I remember going to the clubs and being out in the scene. Chicago isn't a small city, but being in New York City can give you a feeling of awe and "Oh wow, I've never seen anything like this," no matter where you're from. That's exactly how it felt seeing Andre J. out on the town in those early years. They were a popular party promoter and host, and I would see them out in the nightlife scene or sometimes just walking through downtown. They would have this long, bone straight hair and a full beard that made them stand out, even in a New York City crowd. You might catch them in a caftan or a leather skirt and vest. Every element was so distinct. Those images of them have stuck with me even to this day.

The thing that really resonated with me was that Andre wasn't really trying to be a woman. They were just being themself, with what felt most natural to them. It felt natural to have this long, glamorous hair (or sometimes a massive, lush afro) and a full, groomed beard. So they wore it. The closest visual I had ever seen to something like that was the "bearded lady" at a circus. But Andre wasn't some sideshow. They weren't a freak. They weren't seeking attention (even though it came) from anyone. That's just them, and it was perfect.

For them to appear on the cover of French *Vogue* in 2007 with a short bob and beard, photographed with Carolyn Murphy, just affirmed all of this. Every time I appear on the cover of a magazine with my wigs, I feel like I'm working in the same vein. It's my own little homage.

Even though everyone's so used to seeing me with my long hair now, I was taking a risk when I first started wearing my wigs. Whenever you don't look like how people expect you to look, you run the risk of being questioned. And in an extremely visible career like mine, there's the possibility of being judged. Always. The same goes for my clients; there's often such a small gap between a look that gets praised and one that gets criticized. Hunter's feather top, Megan's big natural hair, or even me in drag for *Interview* magazine—a little bit of cowering or lack of confidence could have made any of those looks a disaster.

Innovation is at the core of so many out-of-the-box ideas, and curiosity is a powerful driving force behind that innovation. It's this innate human desire to explore, question, and seek answers that has led to some of the most groundbreaking discoveries and inventions in human history. Curiosity is the pure impulse to pursue a thought, find a solution, seek new possibilities, or stay on a path to see what might be around the next corner. Curiosity often emboldens people to take calculated risks; innovation is, by nature, a risk-taking endeavor. When you leave your assumptions at the door, you'll be poised to learn new things, and perhaps even gain a new perspective.

Curiosity is the key to unlocking a world of wonder and endless possibilities. Embrace it, nurture it, and share your curious journey with the world!

The curious person recognizes that putting yourself out there with an open mind helps form meaningful connections. I personally surround myself with people who I find to be interesting and informed. And when they talk about new things, I listen and ask questions. I'm also constantly scrolling through social media, falling into holes of research on YouTube or TikTok because something has piqued my interest. Curiosity shifts our perspective outward, increasing our capacity for empathy. It is an engine for growth and requires that we embrace uncertainty. *Make curiosity who you are, not something you do.*

THE PATH OF SELF-DISCOVERY

The path of self-discovery is often paved with risks, my friends, and that's where the magic happens! Self-discovery isn't about staying in your comfort zone; it's about venturing into uncharted territory. Taking risks means embracing the unknown, exploring the depths

TAKE ACTION: IGNITE YOUR CURIOSITY

Curiosity is something that can be nurtured and developed. It's easily accessible and readily available to all of us, if we just take the time to cultivate it. With practice, we can utilize curiosity to transform everyday tasks into opportunities for growth or connection. Let's dive into seven incredible ways to ignite your curiosity.

1. **Explore the Unexplored:** Life is an adventure, and there's always something new to discover! Step out of your comfort zone, visit new places, try exotic foods, or learn about different cultures. Keep your passport and your mind open!

2. **Ask All the Questions:** Curiosity starts with asking questions. Don't be shy! Ask "why," "how," and "what if?" at every turn. Dive into conversations, research your passions, and satisfy your inner detective. Keep those questions coming!

3. **Dabble in New Hobbies:** There's a whole world of hobbies to explore, from painting, to cooking up a storm in the kitchen, and maybe even taking up a dance class or two. Trying new things is the best way to discover what sparks your curiosity. So go on, try that random activity you've always wondered about!

4. **Read Widely:** Books are the gateway to infinite worlds and knowledge. Fiction, nonfiction, magazines, blogs—they're all filled with secrets waiting to be uncovered. What will you read next? Share your latest book obsession online, and you might just be surprised what conversations come to life.

5. **Connect with Inspiring People:** Surround yourself with people who inspire you. Seek out mentors and follow thought leaders, and engage in conversations with individuals who share your passions. The people you connect with can be a wellspring of inspiration and knowledge!

6. **Take Notes:** Find a way to make your own scrapbook. Maybe you're like Nick and you want to post inspiring images on your wall or desk, or maybe you keep a separate folder in the albums on your phone. No matter where, create a space that's full of inspiration for you, one that you can easily access daily. When you're reading books or going through old magazines or watching movies, take photos or snippets and put them here, so the space will provide a well of inspiration when you really need it. It's the perfect way to get the wheels going when you're stuck trying to figure out how to complete a new look or project. You can do this with fabric swatches, too.

7. **Curate Your Algorithm**: Everything is so digital today, so it makes sense that inspiration can be as well. No matter what your interest or your vibe, there are pages online dedicated to the thing you love. Give yourself unexpected inspiration and creative boosts through the day by following these accounts and interacting with their content. When you're scrolling through photos from the weekend, trying to procrastinate your next assignment, or you can't figure out what to wear, the perfect clip could come across your timeline to give you the push you need.

of your potential, and unveiling the layers of your true self. It's like setting sail on an adventure without a map, and it's exhilarating!

When you step out of your comfort zone and take those bold steps, you might just stumble upon hidden passions and talents you never knew you had. You might even stumble on a version of yourself you never quite knew existed. Risk-taking allows you to explore various aspects of yourself and see where your true strengths lie. It's like unlocking a treasure chest of potential.

When I think of risks I've taken, my first pair of heels come to mind. They were made for men. I remember them distinctly. As I said before, for years I only wore pieces that I found in the men's section. It could be the most feminine piece possible, but if it was made for men, I would most likely wear it. I'm not sure why, but that's how I shopped for a very long time.

So when Christian Louboutin introduced their first heel for men, I fell in love. Even though I had walked on my tippy toes everywhere while barefoot since I was a child, I had never even thought of wearing something that would raise me off of the ground. But here it was, this spiked shoe about to give me an additional three and a half inches of height. To be fair, that isn't very high for what I wear now, but trust me, it was high enough for me then. I bought them and never took them off.

Those heels felt so natural and so effortless for me. I wore them everywhere. It felt like I had been training my feet all my life to feel this way. So I kept buying more heels, higher and higher. I've never really stopped. What seemed like a risk at first—like would I lose a part of myself, a part of who I am, a part of my unique blend of masculinity— turned into a catalyst for finding myself. And over time I realized this was partially all possible because I had seen people like Miss J Alexander come before me, strutting confidently in the tallest heels.

I watched *America's Next Top Model* religiously in the early days, long before the team knew who I was. Regardless of what you think of her, Tyra Banks really gave us a little peek into the world of fashion, exposing the world to so many facets of the industry and introducing us to many of its important people, season after season. One of the people she introduced was Miss J.

I remember being so impressed with Miss J on the show. He would wear the highest heels with his legs out, teaching the new girls how to strut up and down the runway. More importantly, he was being taken seriously by everyone. He was treated with respect, and his approval was necessary for the girls to progress. This was the first time I remember seeing a feminine man who was regarded highly in this way; Miss J was a businessman who was teaching a skill to others, and his feminine presentation played no part in how he was able to his job.

Ever since I was younger, I've been an advocate of doing your own research.

And I'm not going to lie, I can sometimes be a little skeptical when people talk to me about how great or legendary someone is. Ever since I was younger, I've been an advocate of doing your own research, and this is especially important now more than ever with all the fake news and erasure of certain people's rightful successes. When they would say on the show that Miss J was a big deal in fashion, I went and looked him up. And he was. I read about how he was in Paris at the shows during the era of the supermodels. He worked with designers like John Galliano, Karl Lagerfeld, and Alexander McQueen. He even walked for Jean Paul Gaultier.

He wasn't a drag queen. He wasn't a joke. He was the real deal. The real deal in sky high heels who earned respect from the greats. I kept that image in the back of my head for years. And slowly, when I finally started wearing heels myself, though it felt like a risk, it also meant something to know it was possible. That I could be taken seriously wearing whatever shoe I wanted to wear. I had seen the likes of Miss J do it before, so why couldn't I?

Taking risks can be a learning experience like no other. Whether you succeed or face setbacks, each risk you take is a valuable lesson. Every challenge you overcome, every perceived failure you encounter, it's all part of the journey toward self-discovery. It's like sculpting a masterpiece—each chip and crack adds to your unique story. But having a frame of reference or point of inspiration can really help give you a roadmap that makes you a little surer about your next steps.

Now so much of what I'm doing is about being that point of inspiration for others. I'm writing this book so you can use my experience to help you be more confident. And I live openly and authentically as myself, wearing the hair that makes me feel good and the clothes that make me feel like an icon so people who look like me and have experiences like mine can use me as a way to find themselves. It is the most rewarding part of all of this. Not to be congratulated for being an icon or being influential, but knowing that some little boy in Chicago who I'll probably never hear about is saying, well, if Law Roach can wear that or do this, I can do it too.

And so can you.

"Even if it makes others uncomfortable, I will love who I am."

—JANELLE MONÁE, "Q.U.E.E.N."

O6.

LOVE YOURSELF

've had an interesting relationship with my body for my entire adult life. At my heaviest I was more than one hundred pounds heavier than I am today, and even now my weight can fluctuate month to month. I'm sure that's common for many of us.

But I'm constantly working on injecting more love into that relationship.

Clothing is an interesting addition to our conversations between ourselves and our bodies. Clothing can literally help to shape your body and emphasize or de-emphasize certain parts. The way a piece hugs a specific area might make you feel a little more self-conscious, or the way it squeezes another might make you feel sexy. Clothing can also be a constant reminder of the status of your body. How you fit into a piece can remind you of how you looked at another point in your life. It can really shake you at times and be extremely rewarding at others. And that happens to us all—when I put on a piece that used to be tight and it now feels a little oversized, it does make me feel good. But it's important that we all consciously work to improve those feelings from within.

In terms of magazines, 2021 was a big year for me. I styled thirty-two covers, and five of them featured me! If I'm honest, it's still so surreal that people want me to be on the cover of their magazine. That I've done something or mean something worth highlighting in that way still gives me goose bumps. And while I don't want to go into detail about every cover, one does stand out in my mind.

Every year *Out* magazine puts out their Out100 list, which is a huge deal within the LGBTQ+ community. The list spotlights the movers and shakers in different industries and culture; it always features a group of amazing people doing powerful work. In 2021 I was not only honored to make that list (for the second time), but I also appeared on the cover alongside *RuPaul's Drag Race* season 13 star and winner Symone.

For my solo version of the cover, I decided to go in a new direction for me. Instead of putting couture on and dressing up, I had the idea to strip it down. I went for a more nineties, almost B-boy aesthetic. Think an Adidas track suit, Calvin Klein underwear, and an easy denim jacket. Oh, and don't forget the jewelry. Lots and lots of diamonds— I'm still *Luxury* Law after all. But most importantly, I decided to show off me.

"I'm not perfect and I don't have a perfect body," I wrote on Instagram when I posted the photos. In the cover image I'm holding my jacket open, shirtless with my body for all to see. It was an incredibly vulnerable moment that I was sharing with over one million people. "I've struggled with my weight my entire adult life, even resorting to unhealthy ways to try to stay thin. I decided to be photographed with my shirt off to help me shed some insecurities about my body. FUCK IT this is me."

I remember taking those photos and being a little nervous. I didn't go into the shoot thinking I would be shirtless, it just sort of happened. I don't have a muscular, well-defined body. I have stretch marks and all these imperfections. Even when I go to the beach or to a pool, I've never been the type to have my shirt off—even at my smallest, I've always worn a T-shirt.

But as Micaiah Carter, the amazing photographer, was snapping the photographs, it just felt right. I remember swinging the long braids I was wearing and feeling so free. Micaiah started taking photos of me from behind, and I was there in a Kangol hat with my Adidas track pants pulled down so the top of my Calvin Klein underwear was sticking out and the top of my ass was visible above that. Click. It felt sexy and flirty. I stuck my tongue out. Click.

It felt liberating.

You know, it can be a long time from when you shoot an editorial to when it comes out. I would be lying if I said I didn't have second thoughts afterward about the decisions I made during the shoot. How would my body look? How would it be received? But this was me. The images were shot. I trusted what I felt was right in the moment on set. And I trusted that my tribe would see me for me.

When I finally posted the images, the amount of love that poured in on Instagram was overwhelming. I was in tears from all the supportive comments. While I did it for me and to reconcile some of my own fears, nothing feels quite like people embracing you in whatever form that comes in. It's at that moment that you know people really love you for you, and not this perfected and edited version that doesn't exist.

LEARN HOW TO LOVE YOURSELF

In school we're taught about the whole "nature versus nurture" debate from early on. The age-old question has been about whether people's characteristics are formed by genetics or based on their environment. Many times, I think the life you live is a combination of both.

One part of my self-discovery journey began shortly after my mother's death. I was in my twenties, and I had a long grieving process. Taking the time to properly grieve a loved one or a major loss in your life is important—if you don't, those unresolved feelings may come back up later. I went through a lot of thoughts at that time about happiness and fulfillment, about her life and mine. Sometimes death can do that to you; it can cause you to really consider how to make the most of your time on this earth.

Grief can be a powerful catalyst for self-reflection and personal growth. It often leads us to contemplate the meaning of life and our purpose in it. My mother dealt with chronic depression and struggled with addiction. I think a lot of that is hereditary; we get a lot of our traits and characteristics from our mothers. And as I was doing all of that reflection work, I started to consider how those tendencies had begun showing up in my own life. I worried that I would carry on those traits. Ultimately, I decided that I didn't want to live that way.

I saw how easy it would have been to slip into familiar patterns. I dealt with depression on and off as a teenager and young adult. I don't blame my mother, but I acknowledge how I had begun picking up some of her behaviors for dealing with troubles. It was a legacy I didn't want to repeat, so I made conscious decisions to prevent that. That's the reason I rarely drink at home to this day. I remember watching my mother numb her depression with alcohol, so I rarely allow myself a cocktail at home, though I might have one when I'm out.

The same goes for music. While I love and sort of admire people who seem to have a soundtrack for their lives, playing music when getting ready for work or while in the car is something I don't really do. Having music on like that triggers memories of childhood for me. In our home, music was played mostly when my mother was in a depressive state and was accompanied by her tears.

> By embracing our true identities and sharing them with the world, we own who we are.

After she passed away, I really thought about the person I wanted to be, and I took steps in that direction. Remember, we have the ultimate control over our lives and the choices we make. Often taking those necessary steps requires you to first have a really honest look at yourself. It means assessing what you like, what you don't like, what serves you, what doesn't serve you, and whether you're truly prepared to change those things. It could be something as simple as what's in your closet, or deeper, like the people in your life. In the end, you're worth taking the time and making the effort if it aligns with the person you want to be. It'll help you fall deeper in love with the parts of yourself you already are in love with and increase your appreciation for other parts as well.

I've learned that one of the most profound forms of empowerment we can experience is the control we have over our own lives. It's a declaration that we refuse to be defined by others' expectations or judgments. By embracing our true identities and sharing them with the world, we own who we are. It's transformative, really, and it can carry over into all aspects of our lives.

If you've never been on a red carpet, I can say from experience that it's super intimidating. There can sometimes be hundreds of photographers with flashing cameras, some calling your name, others telling you to turn this way or turn that way, or even to get out of the way so they can take a photo of someone else. All of this is going on while you're trying to pose and be conscious of every single move you make, knowing that each and every second could turn into an image that can become an embarrassing, viral meme on social media. All of this can cause a lot of anxiety.

The secret of getting through the experience is controlling as much of the process as you can. You can't control the fans and you can't control the photographers, so the only thing left is knowing yourself. And the best way to do that is through practice.

I learned this from Zendaya, actually. If you watch your favorite celebrities on the red carpet, they probably have a little routine of poses they do when they get in front of cameras. More likely than not, they practiced them before, alone in front of a mirror. There's a video of Zendaya and me at the photocall for Pharrell's first Louis Vuitton show in 2023. People have commented that we seem in perfect harmony; our poses are perfect reflections of each other. We didn't rehearse that or plan that, but I have been watching her on red carpets for her entire career. I've picked up notes on some of her best, most flattering poses. And I practiced them, in the mirror, watching myself and being honest about what I liked and what I didn't, until I was confident that they were perfect from any angle a photographer could catch me from.

When the hectic energy of the red carpet started, I was able to be as confident as possible on that carpet because I knew myself and what I was presenting. At least I had control over that. This applies to so many areas of your life: taking a long, honest look in the mirror can give you the type of self-assurance that no one can shake.

Confidence is at the core of everything I do. We've already talked about how to begin to build confidence, own your story, identify your authentic self, and continue to push yourself out of your comfort zone. I will never stop reminding you—and myself—that confidence is at the root of everything we achieve. It can be as simple as taking the extra ten minutes in the morning to put on an elevated version of your daily uniform by adding a fun accessory, layering on another piece, or switching out tired sneakers for something more daring. But it's also about knowing yourself: who you are, what you bring to the table, how what you're wearing accentuates you. When you feel good in how you look, that confidence pours out of you and affects everything about your day.

Remember that creating a safe and serene space in your closet is about what makes you feel comfortable, relaxed, and reenergized. You can experiment with different elements, colors, and decorations until you find the combination that resonates with your needs.

TAKE ACTION: BUILDING YOUR SAFE SPACE

It should be clear to you by now that there's so much more to clothes than covering your body. It's a conversation with the world, your confidence, and your own body. It's powerful and should be treated as such. Part of respecting that power begins with not thinking of getting dressed as a tedious task, but as a ritual, even a source of joy.

Every day is not going to be perfect. You might wake up feeling a little down from something that happened the day before. You might be intimidated about what you have on the schedule for later. But whatever it is, your getting ready time is time just for you. If you know it's a day that will be a rough one, getting dressed can be the process of applying your armor and reminding yourself of your intention before going into battle. If you just need to center your energy or boost your confidence after a hectic week, this is the space for that.

When I'm having a tough day, I'll sometimes do multiple outfit changes. Throughout the day, I'll return to my closet, put on a new outfit, and admire myself. I've packed my closets with pieces that bring me joy to see and to wear, so whenever I open the doors, it can really be transformative to my mood. Quick changes always overhaul my energy and have sometimes been key to getting me through stressful days.

Your closet can be a sanctuary for regrouping and resetting your energy when you need it. And it's important that this safe haven really meets you where you are.

- **Embrace Solitude:** Your closet is typically a private space, which makes it an ideal spot to retreat when you need a moment to yourself. You can find solace away from the hustle and bustle of the outside world. Put down your phone and really immerse yourself. This is a time for you, so let all of those notifications wait a few minutes. This can help you focus on introspection, meditation, or simply finding tranquility in the moment.

- **Personalize Your Space:** The physical size doesn't matter—who cares if you have an organized walk-in closet with an expensive chandelier, or the smallest space known to man. You can make whatever you have work for you. Firstly, make sure there's appropriate lighting. Is there a mirror so you can really get into your own beauty and how amazing you look? Are there any little bits of inspiration you can put on the inside of the door? Get creative. What will make it a pleasure to open those doors every day? Go open them now and think of one small change you can make immediately that will tell a story about you.

- **Pamper Yourself:** Find ways to create a luxurious experience in your closet. Think about making space for plush slippers, a soft robe, or your favorite neck massager. Do you have a favorite candle? On particularly stressful days, take a little extra time and care with your process. Light the candle. Breathe it in. Transform your day.

- **Get Organized:** It can be very tough to reset your energy in a messy closet. Knowing where everything is and having a neatly arranged space can promote a sense of order and relaxation. The organization needs to serve you: don't organize it a certain way just because someone else does or says you have to. Think about the way you get dressed and what inspires you. Are you more color driven? Do you generally build your whole look around your pants? What's going to get you excited about getting dressed? Figure out how to organize it in a way that sparks your own interest.

BE HONEST, NOT DESTRUCTIVE

Being honest with yourself doesn't mean being negative or tearing yourself down. It's important that you know the difference. You can acknowledge your differences or who you are without making it a bad thing. As I've already said: your differences can become some of your most powerful attributes. They are what make you unique.

The most confident women I knew growing up were the women in my family. My mother and grandmother were both beautiful and took a lot of pride in their appearance, but they weren't the textbook skinny that was considered "in fashion." And they knew that. But they also weren't trying to be.

I see so many women today who feel badly about themselves and let their confidence slip when they're not the size they think they should be—often it's the size someone else thinks they should be. In our neighborhood if you didn't have a big butt and big breasts, you weren't considered attractive. My mother and grandmother didn't necessarily fit that mold, but that didn't stop them from walking through the world exuding confidence. That confidence was more attractive and went further than any superficial idea of beauty that was the standard. It's from them that I learned this superpower and came to appreciate a wide range of beauty in the people I encounter.

Earlier in my career, I had a rule in styling, and I made sure my assistants adhered to it: we never belittled or spoke negatively of a client's weight. When we had someone who

> Your differences can become some of your most powerful attributes. They are what make you unique.

was not sample size, we'd tell brands "just so you know, she's overs-ample." That was us being honest to get what we needed done while not being destructive or negative about our clients. I would never want to disrespect someone by giving too much importance to their size, and I never have.

As a stylist, it's my job to know my clients' bodies. It makes our relationship all the more intimate. I would never bring up a conversation with anyone about their weight or size, but if a client brought it up, I always tried to handle it with both care and honesty. If a client called and told me, "Hey, I gained a little weight. Would it help if I shed a few pounds?" then I would be honest with them. I would say, "For pictures and television the clothes tend to look better when you're around a certain size." But at the end of the day, it's a personal, individual decision. They get to determine whether a specific image they want to project out to the world is important enough for them to make such sacrifices.

I always follow their lead in having the conversation. And if they decide that change isn't worth it, then I work my hardest to bring the most beautiful clothes and looks to accentuate all of their natural beauty. Because I also know that ultimately, whatever size they are the happiest and most confident at is going to make for the most organic moment on the carpet or at the event.

The thing about being a stylist is that I know what my clients like and what they don't like about themselves. There's no hiding that. I think everybody at some point has experienced insecurity. Even if it seems minor, everyone has hang-ups about their appearance, and depending on the day, it can affect their confidence.

And of course, this doesn't just happen with clients. Sometimes I will look at photos of myself after a night out and even though everyone else may say I looked great, I can see an extra fullness in my face, possibly due to being tired or maybe from a few too many nights drinking at work events. Because of my own personal history with my weight, I immediately see the older version of myself with the slightest body fluctuation. I see the person I was before. Each day I work on this ability to be able to confidently look at myself and everything that I may perceive as a flaw, but I do not let my judgments stop me from stepping out into the world with my best foot forward.

It all ebbs and flows. We can't expect to feel one hundred percent confident in our skin all the time. Loving yourself means that you acknowledge when you're not feeling confident and you allow yourself the grace and time to recalibrate. Be compassionate with yourself. Everyone has moments of self-doubt and insecurity. Rather than being self-critical during those times, offer yourself the same kindness and understanding you would give to a friend or another loved one. You deserve it.

KNOW YOUR WORTH

When I first started as a stylist in Chicago, there was a girl trying to make it as an up-and-coming makeup artist around the same time. The fashion circle in Chicago is small, so we were often booked for some of the same jobs. Things were going well for me, and the jobs were coming in, but over time, I slowly started to see her less and less. This kept happening until eventually I didn't see her at all.

One day I ran into her at an event, and I asked her about it. Where had she disappeared to? The story she told me has stayed with me my entire career. She explained that she had moved back in with her parents, no longer able to afford rent in Chicago. She had become what I now call "the $75 girl."

In those early days, every time I completed a job, I raised my rate. My idea was simple: I did this job, I worked with that client, I'm now more experienced. The next person has to pay for that experience. I would sometimes turn down jobs that couldn't pay the new rate. And

TAKE ACTION: GIVE YOURSELF A FINAL LOOK

Social media sites like Instagram and TikTok give each and every one of us the ability to build our own visual brands. This is happening whether you realize it or not. When someone comes across your feed, the algorithm tells them about you—who you are, what you like, and everything in between. You can be a little more intentional and secure about that storytelling by simply creating a duplicate account. Think of it as a testing ground or beta phase before it goes public. Maybe you use it like a "finsta" and let a few very close friends follow it so they can provide feedback you trust. Maybe you don't need anyone else but want to use it to post a photo and give yourself time to come back to it before you let the masses see it. Give it a try and see if it works for you. Sometimes we can feel just a bit freer knowing no one is watching our every move until we're ready for it.

If you're not really a social media fanatic, there's a way you can bring this into your real life as well. Put a full-length mirror near your door. Make sure getting dressed isn't the last thing you do in your morning routine: get dressed and then eat, or maybe meditate for five minutes. And then when you're about to leave the house, do what I did with Céline Dion for that fateful *Titanic* look—give yourself a final once-over before leaving. Do you feel good? Is there one bracelet you want to slip on? Great. *Now* you look perfect and you know it. Bask in that feeling as you head out into a future with endless possibilities.

that's not always easy. There can be a fear that if you don't take the job that's offered, maybe there won't be another job. But I put my trust in an old phrase my family used to say: "What's for me is for me." Sure, I would make occasional exceptions when I thought the outcome or affiliation would help me in the long run, but I held strong and believed in my own worth.

My makeup artist friend, however, didn't raise her rates. Her prices stayed the same, and she continued to do work as a favor or for experience. When she would tell new clients a new rate, they would respond and say they heard someone else had paid her only $75 for the same thing. She was stuck as the $75 girl. In the end, there wasn't enough money to build a long-term career on.

It's such a metaphor for life. What my makeup artist friend experienced is a common challenge in many industries, and in many areas of life. This is a valuable lesson about self-worth. When you're looking at yourself in the mirror to acknowledge your beauty, make sure you also look yourself directly in the eyes and appreciate what you bring to the table. Be very clear on what your skills and knowledge are worth.

When I moved to LA to try my hand at celebrity styling at the highest level, I knew I needed to take this wisdom to heart. I said to myself: "I'm never going to be the $75 girl." I arrived in LA with a deeply held belief that I was going to be the best. I told myself this daily. I reminded myself that I had the talent and I deserved to be paid well for it. And I knew that it was possible: there were rumors about how much money Rachel Zoe was being paid, and I aspired to her level of success. If anyone disagreed with that aim, then they didn't need to work with me. I wanted to be the best, and I deserved to be compensated for my expertise. And in time (after ten years of hard work and dedication), I achieved what I had set out to do.

Knowing your worth is a testament of self-respect. When individuals acknowledge their intrinsic value, they send a powerful message to themselves and the world around them. This self-recognition boosts confidence and self-assuredness, enabling you to tackle challenges with a positive mindset. It serves as an anchor, grounding you in your self-worth, even in the face of adversity.

Not knowing your worth makes you susceptible to exploitation. In personal and professional relationships, there is a risk of others taking advantage of your skills, labor, or resources without offering proper compensation or recognition. Don't be a $75 girl.

Knowing your worth is also about self-care, so start investing in yourself. It will always be worth it to take a little extra time to make yourself feel good before going out in the world—this means getting ready a little earlier could be the difference in the kind of day you will have. It could mean a spa day and facial to make you feel your best. Or that buying that coat that truly transforms your mood and how you see yourself could be worth it in the long run. If you can afford it, you're worth that investment into yourself.

I do this often—maybe a little too often. I love a great bag and don't mind spending a lot of money on them. But I also know the joy they bring me. Every time I see one of my bags sitting on the table beside me, I feel a little jolt of pleasure. That's worth more than any price tag.

Anything in your life that makes you feel like a better, more confident version of who you are is invaluable. Identify those objects, activities, and people and cherish them forever.

SEEK BALANCE

We're conditioned to look at working all the time as a badge of honor. We were told that if you're not overextending yourself, if you're not working yourself to the bone, if you're not barely making it, if you're not massively sacrificing, then you really aren't being successful. I subscribed to this way of thinking for far too long. I finally realized I had been suffering for success. And then I realized that I didn't want to suffer anymore. I want my success to be linked to my happiness, not my unhappiness.

I spent so many years giving so much of me to my clients and to my career that I couldn't remember the last time I made myself a priority for me. I took very few breaks during my career and would often work through my suffering. As some people say, if you don't stop and take care of your body, your body will stop you and force you to do it. And boy did that happen to me.

The year 2018 was an amazing time of growth in my career. I was working with Zendaya, Céline Dion, Ariana Grande, Mary J Blige, Tom Holland, Anne Hathaway, Demi Lovato, Tiffany Haddish, and Naomie Harris. Zendaya got her first *Vogue* cover, and I was blessed enough that they asked me to be in the shoot. Ariana also was having a major moment and appeared on the cover of

> I want my success to be linked to my happiness, not my unhappiness.

Time and *Billboard* magazines, while Demi covered *InStyle* and Mary covered *Ebony*. I styled those four covers and the music videos for Ariana's "thank u, next" era. Plus, one of the seasons of *America's Next Top Model* that I judged was airing. It was overwhelming. Literally.

"So sad this is my first post of 2019," I wrote on Instagram two days into January. I was posting from a hospital bed. "I've literally been working almost every day for the last 5 or 6 years chasing success. In doing so I've neglected my health, love life, and sometimes my happiness. I've been in excruciating pain for the last month, and I just continued to work through it. Finally, my body and my mind told me enough is enough! I promise 2019 I will learn to put myself first."

If I'm being very honest, I didn't really change much after. Sure, there may have been a temporary switch, but before long I went back to my old habits—in the long run, it became one of the factors in my retirement. Overextending myself has caused a lot of complications for me that I am still dealing with to this day. It's important that you learn from my mistakes and look after yourself. In this case, do as I say and not as I did.

Since announcing my retirement, I've learned a lot about balance. I learned how to truly love myself, and I learned that happiness is a habit that you must work on. It requires just as much attention as the work itself. Balance looks different for everyone. You have to determine what it looks like for you. Right now, for me, it looks like working really hard when I'm working but also truly disconnecting and being off when I'm not. So that might mean two months straight of traveling and doing projects before going on vacation or doing nothing for a month. Maybe for you, it means really doing things that nourish you and that you enjoy every Saturday, or maybe there's a hobby you have that you can do every single day that keeps your spirits up. Whatever it is, you have to experiment and explore what works for your schedule and lifestyle.

Maintaining balance in your life is a powerful way of showing self-love because it prioritizes your overall well-being, health, and happiness—the things no money can buy. Balance involves making intentional time and energy to take care of yourself. This includes getting enough rest, eating nourishing foods, exercising, and practicing relaxation techniques. It also includes setting boundaries with the things that are causing you the most stress, be it your demanding job or a needy family member. The whole work-life balance conversation can start to feel like a lot of babble, but it's truly so important to prioritize this. Take it from me. These acts of self-care demonstrate that you value your physical and mental health, the two ingredients to a happier and longer life.

Overcommitting and overworking can lead to burnout, which is detrimental to your health, happiness, and ultimately your progress. Maintaining balance means recognizing your limits and taking steps to avoid burnout, thereby ensuring your long-term well-being. You aren't going to be able to really feel your most confident if there's a nagging health concern. You can mask it for a little while, but covering it up isn't a sustainable strategy.

Remember, you are your most important asset. Treat yourself with love and kindness, and always remember that self-love is NOT selfish; it's essential!

"Create the highest, grandest
vision possible for your life,
because you become what
you believe."

—OPRAH WINFREY, 1997 COMMENCEMENT
SPEECH AT WELLESLEY COLLEGE

O7.

MANIFEST
AND REFLECT

When I first moved to Los Angeles in 2014, I saw an issue of the *Hollywood Reporter* in a doctor's office. The issue listed the twenty-five most powerful stylists in the business. It's an annual project for the magazine and a big deal in the industry. Holding that issue in my hands sparked such a sense of electricity. I read each entry slowly, savoring the details and imagining myself on the pages alongside these greats one day. I took the issue home with me. It was too important to leave behind.

I had already come to Los Angeles with the goal of being great. I knew I wanted to have a career like Rachel Zoe. But now I had a specific metric of success: I wanted my name on this list that signified the best of the best.

I lost track of that issue itself soon enough, but I never lost sight of that goal. It was in the back of my mind as I built my career.

In 2017, my team got the call from the *Hollywood Reporter* inviting me to be included on that very list, and to be on one of their five covers! It was a dream—a manifestation, actually—come true. On top of this, the honor was historic, as I would be the first Black stylist to appear on the cover. I was photographed alongside two of my favorite clients, Zendaya and Céline Dion. We shot it in an airport hangar, and it was nice to hear Céline talk about how my work with Zendaya had caught her attention.

Nothing fell in my lap, and certainly nothing came easy.

To have these two women who had really made my career take time out of their extremely busy schedules to honor me . . . I was just so grateful. I listened behind the camera as they talked about how thankful they were to have me in their lives, and it almost brought me to tears.

As I waited for our issue to hit newsstands, I wondered if I could find the old issue of the *Hollywood Reporter* that inspired me so much three years before. I looked all over my house for it, and I finally found it under a stack of magazines and books on a nightstand. For all that time, I had slept each and every night with that vision right there next to me.

That wasn't my last time on the list. In 2017 I was on the cover with Zendaya and Céline but listed at number twenty-one on a compilation of the top twenty-five names. I was number nine on the list in 2018, and seventeen in 2019. In 2020, the magazine named me one of the top stylists of the decade, and in 2021 I was named the most powerful stylist in Hollywood, shooting for the cover again. This time I was shot with Zendaya and Anya Taylor-Joy. I made history that year, for the second time, now as the first Black stylist to top the list.

The moral of the story is that I had a vision and a goal. I put out into the universe what I wanted, and then I put in the hard work and didn't give up until I got there. Nothing fell in my lap, and certainly nothing came easy. Even though I didn't see anyone who looked like me that had achieved what I wanted, I kept my eyes on the prize with determination and belief in myself that I could do it.

The secret of manifesting is focus—we all manifest the things that we love and want. So what are you focusing on right now?

MANIFEST DESTINY

I really manifested every single aspect of the person I became. From what I look like—blending those early images I saw of Miss J Alexander and Andre J.—to my career. And not all of these were intentional manifestations, where I had put them up on a mood board and intensely studied a path to replicate. No, most of these manifestations were me taking these mental snapshots of people or things I came across and storing them away. It was this process of meditating on them that made them a part of my destiny.

In my early days, it was Rachel Zoe who I saw as the pinnacle of the ultimate success as a celebrity stylist. So that's who I said I wanted to have a career like: I wanted to be like Rachel Zoe.

I had come across an interview in the *New York Times* where she talked about her career and the work she had done. It was clear: all of your favorite celebrities came to her house (which is where she had her studio) to get the clothes you saw them wearing. It seemed so glamorous, and it was very clearly a large, influential business.

When *The Rachel Zoe Project* came out, we got to see a little more into her world: we got a glimpse into her close relationships with designers and got a sense of the power she held. We watched her cut off the sleeve of a pink Chanel haute couture dress without permission from the brand and her client, Cameron Diaz, went on to become the best dressed person of the Golden Globes that night. I wanted that type of power.

It wasn't that I knew how I would get there. There was no rational thought for me to do anything like that. I wasn't working each and every day thinking I would be exactly like the next Rachel Zoe, but she had shown me something I had never seen before. And without me thinking about it, the universe had begun to put opportunities in my path for exactly that to happen.

I look back over my career now and realize I manifested this for myself. Like Rachel, I did become a stylist of enough importance to receive my own *New York Times* profile—twice. Though I hadn't intended to at the time (but also like Rachel), I became a type of celebrity of my own. I was appearing on television just like her, doing deals similar to hers, and more. These weren't things that I initially set out to accomplish or even imagined I would have the chance to attempt. But as the saying goes: be careful what you wish for. My wish came true in so many unintended ways.

At this point in my life, I feel like I'm a master manifester. I feel like I call into my life what I want, and need, mostly through daily moments of speaking it as if it's already happened. My advice for newbies is that you have to see what you want in your mind's eye and create a feeling and emotion behind it as if you already have it. I manifested success, so I had the opportunity to change my life and change the lives of my family and friends around me. I wasn't running from something; I was running toward something.

The power of manifesting lies in the profound connection between our thoughts, beliefs, and the reality we create. When we set clear intentions, focus our energy, and believe in our dreams, we activate a force within us that can shape our lives.

Manifestation is a process that bridges our inner world with the external universe, aligning our actions and opportunities with our desires. Your thoughts and emotions have the power to shape your reality, and by focusing on positive thoughts and intentions, you can attract and create the things you want.

The true power of manifesting lies in the realization that our thoughts have the capacity to influence the course of our lives and lead us toward the future we envision.

I took a Tony Robbins workshop a couple of years ago, and the biggest thing I learned is that you can trigger your mood. One activity he's known for is having people walk across a path of hot coals. I did it myself, which I can hardly believe. He told us that your first reaction is to think that you'll get burned. That's how we have always been conditioned to respond. In a way, you do manifest the pain—if you've ever taken care of a child, you've likely seen this in action when they begin to cry in anticipation of pain, even if they aren't

TAKE ACTION: HOW TO MANIFEST

Ready to tap into your manifesting powers and create your dream life? I've got you covered with this beginner's guide to manifesting. Get ready to manifest like a pro and attract all the good vibes your way!

Here's how to start manifesting with a few simple steps:

- **Step 1:** Start by getting super clear on what you want to manifest. This could be a specific goal, a new job, better health, a loving relationship, or any other positive change in your life. Write it down in your journal or create a vision board with images and affirmations that represent your desires. The universe loves specificity, so be as detailed as possible!

- **Step 2:** You've got to believe in your power to manifest! Visualize your dreams as if they're already happening. Feel the excitement, gratitude, and joy as if it's all real. Engage your senses and emotions to make the visualization more powerful. This positive energy is like a magnet for your manifestations.

- **Step 3:** Speak it into existence daily to rewire your mindset. Affirmations like "I am worthy of abundance" or "Love flows to me effortlessly" can help shift your energy and align it with your desires. The more you say them, the more you'll believe them! Hype yourself up. If you don't believe it, why would anyone else?

- **Step 4:** Take inspired action. Manifesting isn't just about wishing and waiting without any effort; it's about combining your intentions with proactive steps toward your goal. When opportunities arise, seize them with confidence. Manifestation meets you halfway when you're actively moving toward your dreams.

- **Step 5:** Let go of the need to control. Release the idea that you need to control every detail. Trust that the universe has your back, and your desires will manifest in divine timing. Relax, surrender, and let it flow.

- **Step 6:** Trust the process and be patient. Manifesting doesn't always produce instant results. Maintain faith in your intentions and continue to work toward your goal.

actually hurt. To walk across the coals, though, you have to gain control over your mind and break that thought pattern. It's an exercise to prove to yourself that you're in control of your thoughts and that affects your behavior. The concept of walking across hot coals is a remarkable metaphor for the control we have over our thoughts and emotions. It's all about breaking free from conditioned responses and realizing that our mindset can greatly influence our behavior and, ultimately, our outcomes.

You can teach yourself a word or an action that triggers a change in your mood. Practice using a word or a phrase to break you out of a thought pattern and remind yourself of your power over your mind. Maybe you often feel alone in a crowd or aren't as confident in new spaces that you are in—saying something like "love flows to me effortlessly" can be key in resetting yourself. It can trigger not only a mood change but an entire perspective shift. That shift will allow you to receive and recognize that love as it's being provided. But choose what works for you. By choosing a word or phrase that resonates with you, you create a mental anchor that can help you break free from negative thought patterns and remind yourself of your inner strength. Or simply yell. Yelling can trigger your brain to change the way you're thinking about a situation. I don't yell personally, but I've spent years honing my ability to observe and change my thoughts. Early on in this business whenever I would feel doubt creeping in or I felt unsure, I would tell myself things like

> Manifesting is the power of the tongue. When you speak it, it can and will happen.

"the universe protects and provides" (more on that later) or other affirming mantras. I like to remind myself that whatever situation I'm in or whatever problem I'm facing just isn't that serious. Clearing your brain in this way can really help set the stage for productive manifestation.

THE LAW OF ATTRACTION

I made my own way in fashion, and I'm proud of that. Being a fashion icon isn't just about the confidence you have in yourself; it's about what you pour out into the world. Manifesting is the power of the tongue. When you speak it, it can and will happen. Don't be afraid to ask for the life you want, and more importantly, be confident enough to go after all of it.

There is no such thing as luck. Luck is what happens when preparation meets opportunity. We are the authors of our own destiny— meeting the right people at the right time only pays off if you've put in the time to back up the skills and expertise they've been looking for. Those, my friends, are the keys to the kingdom. We all have the power to have our dream life. Owning that dream is in your power. And you can use it on something as simple as an item of clothing.

Early in my career, when I was living in LA and making my way as a young and eager stylist, I fell head over heels in love with a coat. I was watching the Alexander McQueen spring 2018 collection runway show online and a red leather coat caught my eye. It was bold and immediately gave me butterflies when I saw it. I could picture myself in the supple apple-red leather, cinching the belt around my waist or popping the slightly oversized collar on a windy day. It exuded the raw power that I wanted to harness as I took my career to the next level.

I was in New York shortly after, and I went to the McQueen store to ask about the coat. I knew it was a gamble for a ready-to-wear version to be available, but I wanted to express my interest. The sales-people weren't sure if the piece would even go into production for retail, but they took my information and told me they'd get back in touch. Months later, back in LA, I tried for a second time at another location. Again, the woman there wasn't sure they'd be producing and carrying the coat but said she would check and get back to me. I kept thinking about this coat—I would see it in my dreams occasionally. So when I was in Milan for fashion week months after that, I tried the store there. The salesman gave me the bad news: the company didn't produce the coat for retail. But, he told me, if I really wanted it he could make a special order. At this point, nothing was going to stop me, including the high-priced process of special ordering. I *needed* the coat; I *had* to have the coat. But while he took down my name and information, he didn't follow up. They never reached out about sizing or anything that really would have led to the order happening.

I should have given up by this point, but since we are being honest, I couldn't stop thinking about that red leather. Months later, I was back in LA and I walked into Barneys for a client, and there in front of me was my beautiful, perfect red leather trench coat on a mannequin. Seeing it in person confirmed what I already knew on a cellular level: this coat was meant for me. Except they only had one size in the store and that particular size . . . well, it wasn't for me. And this is to say nothing of the $9,000 price tag. I asked them to hold the piece for twenty-four hours so I could think about it. To spend that much on a coat when I wasn't making all that much as an up-and-coming stylist was a big decision—especially for something that wasn't going to fit correctly.

By the next day, I had shaken my doubts and rushed back to get the piece. With the energy the coat brought me, I knew it would be an investment in myself. But when I went back to the store, it was gone.

The Barneys sales associate said one of his colleagues must have sold it. The worst part: the associate checked the records and found only a few versions of the coat were made, and it seemed that none of the stores had more.

Weeks later, I was in New York City and had basically given up. I was shopping for a client and running through the men's section at Barneys, and there it was. The red Alexander McQueen leather coat. My coat. And it was in my size and 40 percent off. There was no way I would let this moment pass me up after letting it sit in my head for almost a year. I immediately took the coat to the register to buy it— *yes! It's finally mine!*—and the sales associates recognized me. With a wink, he told me that in just a few days the coat would go from 40 percent off to 60 percent off. So I waited those couple of days, in awe that after so long I would finally have it, and then I bought the coat of my dreams.

That experience with the coat underscored the power of the law of attraction. Even though I stopped wearing the coat years ago, I keep it in my closet to remind myself of how it came to me. The power behind the law of attraction is ultimately love. You attract things into your life that you love, and I loved that coat. Ever since the first time I saw it walk down the runway, I kept looking at the picture. I kept asking about it. I never stopped thinking about the coat. And eventually I manifested that coat into my life. When the time came to make the purchase, I was ready.

That red leather coat made me feel like the bold, successful stylist man I knew I was. It was an investment in myself and in my confidence. It was worth the price tag because I was worth it. And the universe brought it to me as a result of my unending desire.

Just as you can attract the things you love and desire, you can also attract negativity if you focus on it. The law of attraction is based on the principle that like attracts like, so the energy and thoughts you emit into the universe can draw similar energy and experiences back to you. Be careful about what you obsess over.

If you consistently focus on negative thoughts, fears, doubts, or feelings of lack, you are more likely to attract negative experiences or situations into your life. This is why it's important to be mindful of your thoughts and emotions, as they can influence what you manifest.

By cultivating positive thoughts, practicing gratitude, and maintaining a hopeful and optimistic mindset, you can attract more positive experiences and opportunities into your life. It's all about consciously directing your thoughts and emotions toward what you want to manifest and steering away from what you don't want.

I'm such a huge fan of Diana Ross—she's beautiful, stunningly stylish, and extraordinarily talented. I watch her old interviews a lot, and there's one from 1976 where she is promoting her film *Mahogany*. After hearing her talk about the amazing way she has set up her life, consisting of a fulfilling family life with her children as well as a great professional life as an actress and performer, the interviewer asked her what she would do if there's an accident or something doesn't go according to plan. I think about her response a lot.

"I have a certain positiveness about my life, but I realize that every time I create a positive thought in my mind, I also create a negative thought," she says. "It's just like 'I'm going to be very successful' and my mind says 'oh no you're not.' So since I create positive and negative, it's which one I give the most attention to that is powerful. When I think positive constantly, it's very powerful. It controls me. If I think negative all the time, it's going to control me too. So right now my positive thought is there is going to be no disaster to destroy what I have planned for me and my family, and if there is, that's life."

I think about this interview a lot because I agree with Diana. I feel her meaning. Life happens but it does not benefit any of us to ruminate on the negative possibilities. Our thoughts have power not only in our perception of the world but on the energy we send out and attract. So take stock: Are you giving more attention to the positive or negative?

GET YOURSELF AN ATTITUDE OF GRATITUDE

In a world where the next big thing is just a scroll away, it's easy to forget the simple yet profound practice of gratitude. Take it from me: gratitude is not just a buzzword or a fleeting trend; it's a life-altering mindset that can usher in immense positive change. The power of gratitude transcends the boundaries of screens and hashtags, reaching deep into our hearts and lives, bringing about connection, abundance, and fulfillment.

Gratitude isn't just about saying "thank you" for the good stuff; it's a mindset, a way of life. At its core, gratitude is an attitude, a way of perceiving the world. It's about recognizing and appreciating the goodness that exists within and around us, regardless of our circumstances. When you embrace gratitude, you attract more positivity, abundance, and love into your life. It's like a magnet for all the good vibes the universe has to offer. Gratitude is how you keep the positive energy flowing.

Every day, take a moment to say thank you for things big and small. Feel the warmth of appreciation in your heart and watch as your world transforms. When you live in a state of gratitude, you not only create a life filled with joy and fulfillment, but you also inspire others to do the same.

Be grateful for who you are and what you have at this point of your life. I never say, "I hate this body" because I know the work it took me to get here. Love yourself in all states of yourself, and be grateful for the place you are now.

Be grateful for the setbacks and for the conflicts. They shape who you are, they push you to evaluate situations and relationships and where you put your energy.

Be grateful for the things that you don't get. The job that you thought that you wanted but didn't get is actually a gift. It's the universe course-correcting you in the direction that you need to be going in. This can be a powerful perspective shift. It's often challenging to see the silver lining in missed opportunities or unfulfilled desires, but in many cases, they are actually blessings in disguise. When a job or opportunity you thought you wanted doesn't materialize, it could be a sign that the universe has a different plan for you, one that aligns more closely with your purpose and personal growth. It may redirect you to a path that is more in line with your passions, values, and long-term aspirations.

I often say that my career was a trial by fire, where I had to prove myself by learning on the job, in real time. When I began to work I had very little experience as a celebrity stylist, so I started to work with a lot of clients during this period. This allowed me to gain a lot of experience in a very short period of time and prove to people I was no one-trick pony. There were nights on some red carpets where I would have ten or more looks. And because I have this wide view of beauty, my clients were of varying sizes, with completely different aesthetics. It was not easy: I worked tirelessly to make sure that each and every person I worked with felt cared for and happy. I'm a people pleaser at heart; working in the service industry, it's always been important to me that every single person who worked with me has felt like they got exactly what they paid for, if not more.

But no matter how hard it was, what I learned in that crash course of about four years became invaluable as my career began to flourish. I drew on every single one of those hard-earned lessons from what some may have called the worst part of their careers. In 2021 I went to the Met Gala and styled eleven people, not including myself, and it was one of the world's most discussed red carpets. I had the honor of styling the likes of Chance the Rapper and his wife, Hunter Schafer, Lewis Hamilton, Addison Rae, Alton Mason, Kehlani, and more. It was another history-making night.

> I knew what it was like to work with so many clients and only have so many resources but still get the job done.

The Met Gala is a fund-raiser for the Metropolitan Museum of Art's Costume Institute. To raise money, sponsors like large fashion brands buy tables and invite celebrities to sit with them. As a result, most of the designers on the red carpet there are major labels that can afford to buy the seats.

When Lewis Hamilton and I were discussing his options for going, we decided to do something different. Instead of being invited by a brand, Lewis paid for a table himself, and we identified a group of young Black designers to come with him. We were using Lewis's platform to spotlight these amazing creatives who otherwise couldn't afford an opportunity like this. I worked with the designers and the guests each of them came with, styling each of the looks in the months leading up to the red carpet. The day of, I even made it a point to see each and every one of them, going between the four hotels they were split between to give them some one-on-one time.

It was a hell of a lot of work, and it was only possible because I had gone through the fire all those years ago and had come out on the other side. I knew what it was like to work with so many clients and only have so many resources but still get the job done. For that, I was and still am grateful.

In moments like these, it's essential to trust the universe and believe that there's a reason behind every twist in your journey. These apparent setbacks or even moments where you feel like you're getting the shorter end of a stick in a deal can lead to unexpected, rewarding opportunities that you might not have discovered otherwise. So don't fret if you're going through the fire right now; you too will come out the better for it.

MAKE THE TIME TO REFLECT

Taking the time to reflect is an absolute game-changer. Reflecting on your experiences can lead to personal growth and self-awareness. It can also encourage you to see patterns, make connections, and gain a broader perspective on your own life. This was a key piece of advice from Godmother Eunice; though she gave me that initial wisdom about getting in the stadium, the catalyst to my relocating to Los Angeles, she also gave me one of the most important lessons in my life. She taught me the power of being still, and how it can allow you to reflect and be purposeful about your next steps.

At the end of my career as a stylist, I was living my dream. Everything I manifested for myself professionally, I had achieved. But what I didn't understand when I was writing those mental lists was the importance of my inner self. I had no boundaries, and no self-care practice.

I had been committed to my work for so long, but I never understood the concept of putting myself first, which I think a lot of entrepreneurs are guilty of. A few years ago, my uncle passed away, and I wasn't able to go to the funeral because of work commitments. I reached out to his daughter to see if she could change the date of the funeral. In hindsight, I'm mortified that I asked her that, and regretful that I didn't prioritize myself and my family over my work. Instead of me trying to move a funeral to accommodate me, why didn't I just change my schedule to accommodate the funeral? I missed a lot of important moments over the years but vowed to never let it happen again.

I used to laugh at people who talked about rest and self-care. My mentality lauded self-sacrifice and martyrdom of working above all else. I would say, "I haven't slept in two days," or "I've been in Paris three times in one week" as a badge of honor. I thought if you didn't overwork yourself, then you weren't working hard enough.

For so long, I had been working like my life depended on it. If you have never experienced being a child who has had to go to bed hungry, you will never understand the reason why I was working the way I was. I still wake up every morning with that gut-wrenching feeling that this can all be over in an instant, and I will have to go back to where I came from. So that's the reason why, in my own mind, I felt like it was OK to put myself on the back burner for everybody else. I feel I have to work harder and be better than everybody else. I often think about that little boy who went to bed crying because there just wasn't enough food for me to be full. No matter how much success or financial security we achieve, that feeling of "what if" never goes away.

I'm proud of my career, but I'm not proud of all the other things. I'm not proud of pushing myself to the point of exhaustion and illness. For a couple of years before my retirement, I was sick. I went to doctor after doctor who couldn't find anything wrong. I could barely walk some days. But no matter what, I still got up, got on that plane, and went to work.

Now that I've started to re-prioritize myself again, I'm the happiest I've ever been in my entire life. I've learned the hard way that while your career is undoubtedly something to be proud of, it's crucial to recognize that self-sacrifice and burnout are not the price tags we need to attach to our accomplishments. Pushing yourself to the point of exhaustion and illness is not the way to greatness. Your well-being, physical and mental health, and overall happiness should always come first.

It's time we all reframe our definition of success. Ultimately, it's about achieving your goals, making a difference, and living a fulfilling life, all while taking care of yourself and finding balance. It's not about doing as much as you can as fast as you can. Of the many things I'm thankful for, I'm so thankful that success found me at this point in my life. If it had happened any earlier, I don't think I would have been able to appreciate and enjoy it as much as I do now. My success and my gift of discernment came to me at the right time.

In art, in creation, in culture, in business, there is a constant need for questioning everything. Reflection is the compass that keeps you on course in the vast sea of opportunities. It's that pause button that lets you step back and take a good look at where you are, where you've been, and where you're headed. I hope you can look back on all that you've achieved with gratitude for the person you were, but also look forward with anticipation for the version of you that awaits.

"You have to believe in yourself
when no one else does."

—SERENA WILLIAMS, 2020 SPEECH AT
MOURATOGLOU ACADEMY

08.

THE
RENAISSANCE ERA

To be reborn, you must first let go of everything.

My retirement post was sent into the universe while I was on the way to the airport for the Hugo Boss Fall/Winter 2023 runway show in Miami.

When I arrived, I went right to the fitting. I was still raw and on an emotional rollercoaster as I processed the reality of my retirement, and I was walking into the hectic storm that happens with fashion events. I walked into a situation where everybody at the fitting had seen the news. I was seeing the comments and calls that were pouring in on my phone in real time. It was overwhelming, but everyone on set was supportive, and I absorbed all the love I was receiving.

Pretty early into my fitting, Naomi Campbell, who was also walking the show, summoned me to her dressing room. She was so loving and encouraging, but she urged me to reconsider. And by urged, I mean she told me to take down my Instagram post immediately. She got Edward Enninful, who was at the time the editor in chief of *British Vogue*, on the phone, and they both told me I could get through this tough season. They wanted

> I felt so seen and so cared for, and yet, I still felt like I was making the absolute right decision for myself.

me to know that they were behind me all the way, and that my voice was vital and necessary within the industry. It became an incredibly meaningful time, with these two fashion icons whom I deeply admire telling me how much they supported me no matter what. I felt so seen and so cared for, and yet, I still felt like I was making the absolute right decision for myself.

The show itself was happening the next day, merely thirty-six hours into retirement. My team was there as I was getting ready, helping me prepare to go on the runway. It was different from normal, of course, because I was the talent this time. I wasn't doing final touches on someone else, making sure they felt as good as they looked—my team was doing that for me (and of course, I was doing it for myself).

This was my first major runway show, my debut, but I wasn't nervous. In my head, I'd been walking the runway my entire life. I'd always treated the hallways of my school, the streets of Chicago, New York, or LA like my own personal runway, and believe me, I know how to walk. And it wasn't just any show. I was up there with Naomi, Pamela Anderson, and Precious Lee. I was among supermodels and A-list celebrities. Names of that caliber can make anyone stand up just a little bit taller, no matter how confident you are.

Typically, I would have been overjoyed at the experience. But as you can imagine, I had a lot on my mind, and I felt heavy with the emotions of the previous two days. I saw this runway show as an incredible opportunity and a chance to have fun. It felt like a new beginning to me. I wasn't just walking down the runway; I was standing on my own, walking into a new future. Some people thought I had organized the timing this way on purpose, but that's just not true. I had been in conversation about the Hugo Boss show for months. And when I retired, I was thinking of nothing else but freedom. The universe brought the two together as if they were the perfect ending to a fairy tale.

The show was gorgeous, and the catwalk was outside with this magnificent water feature in the center. There were colored lights in the water fountain, blues and purples strobing in time with the music. The lights were bold against the dark sky. It was windy that evening, and when the wind blew, we could feel the spray from the fountain. It felt like a baptism. They put me in a gorgeous cream-colored suit, and it truly felt like my moment of rebirth. It was a spiritual experience. When I was walking, the water hit me, and I put my hands up and ran my fingers through my hair. I felt like the universe was speaking to me in that moment, telling me I'd made the right decision, holding me as I walked into my new, bright future.

THE POWER OF A SECOND ACT

There are many chapters to every book. Reinvention is the compass guiding us through uncharted territories, reminding us that we are not bound by the chapters already written. To redefine our stories, we must find the strength to discard what no longer serves us and embrace the unfamiliar with open arms. The power of reinvention lies not only in the act itself but in the liberation to become the fullest, most authentic version of ourselves.

Life is about reflection and reinvention. Don't stagnate. Don't lose that spark. Continue to evolve and push yourself. Embracing change and pushing yourself out of your comfort zone not only keeps things interesting but also allows you to discover aspects of yourself and the world around you that you might have otherwise overlooked. The power of reinvention is that it allows us to shed the skin of the past and emerge as the architects of our own evolution.

Lindsay Lohan has had such a long career. From *The Parent Trap* in the 1990s to movies like *Life-Size*, *Freaky Friday*, and *Mean Girls*, we can all agree her films are true classics. The world has really watched her grow up, in a way, through her work on-screen. Working with her would be major for any stylist.

When we first worked together, I was hired to style a commercial that Lindsay was involved in. It wasn't a big deal, but it did allow us to meet each other properly. I think it's what led her to request that her team hire me for the press run of her Netflix film *Falling for Christmas* in 2022.

Media called that press tour the beginning of Lindsay's renaissance moment. If I'm honest, that's what it felt like to me too. She was no longer a child star or teen actor, but a woman ready to take on a new adventure. She would show up on time or early to every meeting or fitting. She was always super professional and came into rooms with a smile as if she was genuinely happy to be there. She seemed grateful for every moment and excited about the opportunities it would bring. And that was the version of Lindsay I wanted to make sure the public knew.

The most discussed look we did was our first: a color-blocked Akris suit, gold earrings, and platform heels from Giuseppe Zanotti. It was easy, fun, and professional without being matronly. It felt like the adult version of the Lindsay that we all watched grow up. (The same could be said for a perfectly sculpted leather Versace dress I put her in for a Jimmy Fallon appearance.) And it was a fashion-forward look: people forget that this starlet is a true student of fashion with a deep knowledge of clothes. (Though it didn't work out in the end, there was a reason she was named the artistic director of Ungaro in 2009 at just twenty-three years old.) In that way, it felt like I had a collaborator, someone to bounce ideas off of. She had all these close relationships with designers (she was once a muse to Karl Lagerfeld), which was impressive in and of itself, but what I loved even more was that we were able to have real conversations about the clothes we were envisioning, what they said, and the stories we wanted to tell through them. The story was simple: Lindsay was back. And the people heard it.

I'll repeat it: you have the power to create your future. How many times have you wished you could change something about your life? How many times have you wanted a second go? Maybe you feel unfulfilled. Maybe you feel "happy enough." Maybe you just want to challenge yourself. Whatever the reason that drew you to picking up this book, it's truly the first step to making a change. If there is a part of you that has become complacent, bored, unhappy—embrace it, OWN IT, and let's change that. Stop waiting to reach your goal weight, find the perfect man, or land that promotion to live a life you love. Life is meant to be lived, not survived. I promise to take you on a journey that will awaken parts of you that have laid dormant for years. So no more excuses. Stay eager. Be grateful. The time is now.

The first step—and believe me, this may be the hardest—is to understand in your gut that *you deserve it*. You deserve to be truly happy and content with your life, not just mostly happy, or OK, or getting-by-just-fine-thanks. You *deserve* to feel good about your body, your business, and everything you invest your time and energy into. You deserve to look how you want and to feel confident walking through life. But to do all of that, sometimes you've got to be willing to pivot when something isn't working. Don't bang your head against the wall expecting something else—or someone else—to change. Sometimes when I haven't been satisfied with how certain aspects of my life were going, I've had to take the (hard, challenging, but worthwhile!) steps to pivot, reframe, and change what wasn't working until I felt truly happy.

So, here's to the constant journey of self-discovery, to the evolution of ideas, and to the courage to reinvent yourself when the story takes an unexpected turn.

THE UNIVERSE PROTECTS AND PROVIDES

I use mantras a lot. I find they can be the perfect way to change your mood or your perspective in real time. If you're feeling a little insecure, tell yourself that you are powerful and confident. You are the best at what you do. You may need to start doing this out loud, in the mirror, but over time it's something you can recite to yourself mentally in a time of need. I rely on my mantras so much, reciting them in my head, that they often work their way into things I'm saying to others. I do this so much that people around me are influenced by it, adopting the idea into their own life. I have no better example than with my mantra, "The universe protects and provides."

This is something I repeat to myself every day. When an opportunity I was looking forward to doesn't materialize, or when someone randomly reaches out to work with me at the same time I really needed their specific sort of assistance: "The universe protects and provides."

To me this means that the universe will protect me from everything that could come into my life and disrupt or disturb what I have going on, and that the universe also provides me with everything that's meant for me. It will provide me with all the tools to manifest my dreams and pursue my purpose. I like the idea that there's a higher power looking out for us, no matter what you believe that power to be. So when you don't get what you want or things don't work out the way you expected, it's the universe protecting you for the things that are coming. Be grateful for that.

"The universe protects and provides."

It's like the universe, with its cosmic wisdom, sees the bigger picture and orchestrates events in our favor. What may seem like a setback or disappointment in the moment is actually a cosmic redirection, steering us away from paths that wouldn't lead to our ultimate fulfillment. It's as if the universe has our backs, intervening to ensure that we align with the opportunities and experiences that will truly nourish our growth and happiness. Trusting this process can be challenging, but every time a project that didn't materialize for me turns out to be something different from what it originally appeared, it gets easier.

I'm living the reality of that mantra in this moment. Retiring from a career I've dedicated a decade to is no easy feat. It was truly one of the greatest acts of confidence in my life. To walk away from a sector of the industry where I had become a real cornerstone, that others had called me the "most powerful" in, was tough. But when I was dealing with the teams of my clients—the layers of managers, agents, publicists, assistants—and the conference calls, big personalities, scheduling, and rescheduling, it was increasingly difficult to maintain my wide-eyed wonder at fashion. And so I took a risk.

I use the term risk with a caveat—there's a big asterisk there. I was taking a risk, but I knew in my core that the universe would protect and provide for me. I would repeat that to myself in my lowest moments: I know I'm making the right decision. The universe will protect and provide for me. And it has.

The Hugo Boss show really could have been the end of me, one final hurrah as they say. But that baptism was the start of a new chapter that has only made my career grow. Afterward I was asked to host the British Fashion Awards red carpet, which was a major sign to me that the industry still valued my voice. I was approached to be a permanent judge on the new reality competition *OMG Fashun* with Julia Fox, which allowed me to continue doing the work of discovering and mentoring the next generation of fashion designers, something I've done my entire career. And there's this book, where I'm still making fashion icons, one person at a time, starting with you.

The decision to retire was about protection—protecting my mental and physical well-being. I took time off to address some important things going on with my body that I had been neglecting over the years as I catered to the needs of clients. And everything that has come after, every opportunity and every red carpet, every brand deal and chance to tell my story, has all been the universe providing moments for me to fulfill my purpose in this new way.

Over the years, I've shared this mantra with people, and I love to see how they use it in their own lives. I shared it with Zendaya when she was just sixteen years old, and she really took to it. We will say it to each other in a moment when it's needed—if a deal doesn't come through or if something feels impossible. In fact, she had a birthday party a few years ago with a big wooden art installation as the center-piece. I sadly couldn't make it, but people sent me photos and videos. "The universe protects and provides," the installation read. She was honoring this little thing I taught her in such a sentimental way. A few weeks later, I learned that the installation came in two parts: Zendaya kept the section that says, "The universe protects," and she sent me the other half that says "and provides." I cherish that piece as a symbol of our relationship to this day.

And it's also a constant reminder that no matter what happens, the universe truly has my back.

WHAT ARE YOU CHASING?

While it's important to have goals and direction in your life, what's most important is confidence. You don't need to know *how* you're going to get there; you just need to know where you want to be.

Drop me anywhere, in any situation, and I'll be the best. If I wasn't a stylist and I was a dentist, I would be one of the best dentists in the world. When I was a bartender, I was one of the best in my city and my community. I made the most money and I had the most regulars who would come to see me where I worked. I'm going to be the best in whatever I do, and I really believe that. That's confidence. Once you develop your confidence, you can do anything you want. And you can wear anything that you want. Any path is open to you when you believe in yourself.

I know I can do anything. In the future, I want to make documentaries and feature films. I feel like there are so many stories that I can tell. I'm dreaming about my acceptance speech for the awards that will come as a result of this work. I know it already—I see it so clearly. By the time this book is released, I may have already started on a project.

Belief in yourself is like having the master key to unlock countless doors of opportunity. You are capable and you are deserving, and never let anyone tell you differently. Believing in yourself is not just a mindset; it's a catalyst for turning dreams into reality. It's the fuel that propels you forward, breaking down barriers and turning challenges into stepping-stones.

In the hustle and bustle of life, it's easy to get caught up in the chase without pausing to reflect on what truly fuels our ambitions. Are we chasing external validation, societal expectations, or our authentic passions? Ask yourself: "What am I chasing?" This question prompts reflection, encouraging us to stop and deeply consider our motivations and highest desires. It challenges us to evaluate whether the chase is a meaningful quest for personal growth and fulfillment or a sprint toward fleeting external markers of success. Ultimately, understanding what we are chasing empowers us to navigate our paths with intention and authenticity, ensuring that the pursuit is a genuine reflection of our inner compass.

I know firsthand how feeling stuck or uninspired can really cause a downward spiral. In my earlier days, August was always a slow month for me. I'm not sure if it was just the fashion business in

You are capable and you are deserving, and never let anyone tell you differently.

general or something going on with the cosmos, but it was always slow. There was just something about that month. I could have an amazing year and then August would come. It got so bad that I started to expect it every August. June and July would come and I would think, well, I need to prepare for this bad August coming up. What I didn't realize at the time was that I had begun to manifest that.

So I started talking to myself, like I've encouraged you to do. Every time I would say "Oh, August is around the corner, my worst month," I would counter that thought by thinking: *August is going to be just as good as July. July is going to be better than June.* And that's exactly what would end up happening.

I use this sort of positive thinking to escape feelings of being stagnant. That feeling of inertia is the worst when you want to move up the ladder, get ahead, get out of a relationship, or just make a simple change in your life. When the smallest things seem like a massive challenge, we do what any human does: we give up, we make excuses, and things just stay the same. But it's only you who can initiate the change to start the momentum going in another direction.

Use the lessons we've gone over in this book to do that. Check in with yourself and remind yourself of your goals consistently. Check what sort of self-talk you're engaging in and change it as you need to. If none of this seems to be working and you're in the need of a hard reset, consider stepping into a new renaissance era. Follow along to find out exactly how.

TAKE ACTION: STEP INTO YOUR OWN RENAISSANCE ERA

Growth is the way forward. Life is about continually progressing and evolving, refining your way to become the best you. For a select few people, their growth might just be a straight, consistent line: they have always been going toward this one fixed point in the future, or maybe they've always had a very narrow, specific view of how they've wanted to show up in the world. But for many of us, this trajectory changes and evolves as we do. We may shift direction, sometimes completely, and dust ourselves off for new adventures once we realize something is no longer serving us or is leading us somewhere we didn't intend to go. And the best way to do that is going through a renaissance era, a period of growth and renewed energy.

This book, in totality, has really been about accessing that renaissance era to start you on the path to being a fashion icon. It's been about accessing a new rush of excitement about life and about who you are. Here, we put it all together to jumpstart your next chapter.

1. **Remind Yourself of Who You Are**. Remember, it's truly all about confidence. You know who you are. You know what you excel at. You know your core competencies. Remind yourself of those things. Sure, you may be trying out a new look or a new career, but you've done it before. You can do it again because you're just that good. Stand strong in that as your foundation. Go to a mirror and tell yourself about your strengths if you need to—and don't be shy about it. If you can't acknowledge it, who will?

2. **Get an Idea of Where You're Going.** If you're wanting to enter a renaissance era then that means you've been looking for a switch up. Something has not been working. Once you've reaffirmed who you are, it's important to get a sense of where you want to go. Are you hoping for a new look? What's the general direction you're hoping to go in? Maybe your last look can tell you what you don't want. It's not important that you know exactly where you're going, but having a general direction is important. For example, you might not know the exact home you want to live in, but getting a sense of the state, or even the city, can help you narrow down on your decision.

3. **Start on Your Path.** This process is going to be different for everyone. Some of you are going to be like me; you'll want to jump in headfirst. It's like when I decided to move to Los Angeles to pursue my career as a stylist or when I retired with no preparation. That's the type of person I am: if I'm going in for a haircut, I want a big chop. But maybe that's not you. Maybe you just want to take a few inches off now and then a few inches off later. Maybe you want to slowly start integrating these new changes into your current style, trying them out bit by bit. You want to develop a level of comfort with them as you slowly transition your style over. That's fine. Do whichever works best for you, but you have to start the journey, step by step.

4. **Walk with a Slight Air of Delusion.** Be careful about what you're manifesting. While some would encourage you to prepare for setbacks and to stay on the lookout for obstacles, I encourage you not to give any brainpower to that.

Save all your energy and thoughts for the positive. Walk with an air of delusion; there will be no delays and only green lights all the way. Manifest that into your future. Know innately that you are deserving of good things and that the universe will protect you and provide in times of need. And be confident that should something arise, you are capable of handling it no matter what.

5. **Curate Your Algorithm.** If you're switching up where you're headed, it might be time to do an audit of what you're pouring into yourself. Are the environments you find yourself in and the images you find yourself obsessing over related to your new destination? What about books? Are you acquiring more information about your new vision so you can feel more confident about seeing yourself there? Go follow five accounts on social media that are specific to this new vision you have, to make sure that little by little you are finding inspiration throughout your day.

6. **Share Your Dreams Widely.** Some people believe in not talking about what you're doing until it's done. "Work in silence," they say. Not me. I believe in sharing your hopes and dreams with other people and talking about what you're planning. It's a way of manifesting to say it out loud. This is how you speak it into the universe and create a vibration to make it come true. And you never know how that person could help you. Maybe you tell a friend that you're looking to move your own style in a more eye-catching direction, and they know the perfect store, or even have some pieces they want to give to you. Or maybe they know someone who knows someone looking to finance a

project just like yours. Talk about your vision and watch the connections flourish.

7. **Bask in Your New Era.** When you begin to make these changes, it's important to congratulate yourself. See how these adjustments feel—are the results what you had hoped for? Make adjustments as necessary and revel in your successes when they occur. This should strengthen your confidence and help you move forward in an even bolder way. Remember, this is you, a person of your own creation. You have determined your desires and then manifested your own destiny.

HOW TO LIVE YOUR BEST LIFE

I remember in high school there was a state standardized test. The school only administered the test to people who they thought were college bound. My best friend at the time was super smart—she ended up graduating valedictorian. We were an interesting pair: if she was ranked number one in the class, I was number three hundred out of three hundred.

When this test came around, it was a given that she be offered a chance to take it. I was not, and that offended me. It offended me so much that I asked around about it. I'll never forget it. School administration said they only wanted to give the test to people who they thought were going to pass and who they believed were capable of getting into college. I thought that was so fucked up. I've always had something rebellious about me. I protested, and they ended up letting me take the test. And that one test changed the trajectory of my life. Tip: never bet against me.

When the results came back, one of the teachers ended up giving my friend my results along with her own. "You ended up scoring higher than me!" she said when she came to tell me the numbers. "And you're the one that people think won't do shit." In that moment, I realized I can do whatever I wanted to do if I set my mind to it. No matter what anyone said, no matter what any institution thought, no matter how the cards were decked against me, I knew I could do anything. Doing better than what the administrators expected gave me a bedrock of confidence that serves me to this day. This unshakeable self-assurance means I'll never let anybody—and I mean *anybody*—tell me what I can and cannot do.

Because of that test, I went to college, which gave me tools I would use later on in my career. And I came back to that same attitude and confidence when I entered the styling industry: I didn't look like the women who were succeeding at the highest levels, like a Kate Young

I'll never let anybody—and I mean *anybody*—tell me what I can and cannot do.

or a Rachel Zoe. But I wasn't going to let that tell me what I could do or who I could be.

I can do whatever I want to do. And that applies to you as well.

Each of us has within us the ability to do or be whoever we want. If you don't see someone who looks like you wearing the clothes you want to wear, don't let a lack of confidence hold you back: go do it anyway. If you think it's time for a radical career change because you have a uniquely amazing vision you're not seeing anywhere else: go pursue it. People will give a laundry list of reasons why you can't accomplish a goal: because you weren't born into the right family, because you didn't go to the right school, because you don't have the right amount of money, because you didn't get the right scores. Fuck them. Become the person you wish to see in these spaces.

Take a moment to yourself, speak your destiny, and then show them who you are. I, for one, cannot wait to meet this version of you.

CONCLUSION

The journey toward confidence, self-expression, and style culminates with a clearer picture of who you are and what kind of mark you want to leave on the world. Becoming a fashion icon is not about the clothes you wear but rather the way you carry yourself through the world. Yes, you can curate a wardrobe that tells the world about you and gives them a sense of the person wearing the clothes, but ultimately, it's about how those pieces make you feel about yourself that matter most.

This book was intended to be a resource, a boot camp of sorts to help you find out about yourself and who you are—you'll notice there isn't one "no whites after Labor Day" sort of style mandate. I hope you will see it as only the start and will continue your style and life evolution with creativity, self-assurance, and a touch of audacity, because it's what you deserve. And I hope more than anything that you will carry with you the inspiration to fearlessly express yourself, embrace your uniqueness, and confidently stride through this world as the one-of-one creation that you are. Come back to these lessons and to the exercises as you need to, whenever you need to refine your technique or need a dash of support. But remember that the path to fashion icon status is a personal one—it's an exploration of self-discovery and self-love through clothing.

I believe everything you do in your life is a step forward meant to lead you to the next destination. My grandmother's passion led me to vintage clothes, vintage clothes led me into styling, and then styling led me to celebrity styling and fame of my own. And this led me to write this book and share myself (and these tips) with the world and you. Who knows where I'll go from here. I do know that I want to be more involved with people who look like me and who want the opportunity to do things that I've done. I want that to be my legacy. I want to help change people's lives—and not just my celebrity clients. This book is only the first step of that journey.

As you embark on the hard work to change your life, you're probably wondering how you'll know when you've actually gotten there. Well, you'll *definitely* know. You'll feel it in your bones. You'll have a sense of accomplishment; you'll see the changes in your daily life that you've always been dreaming of. But know that the true win starts before you make any real acts; it's all wrapped up in the confidence you've been cultivating since day one.

So, tell me—no, tell the world—are you confident enough to call yourself a fashion icon yet?

"Becoming a fashion icon is not about the clothes you wear but rather the way you carry yourself through the world."

ACKNOWLEDGMENTS

This book would not have been possible without the love and unwavering support of the following people: Zendaya, Céline Dion, Ariana Grande, Kerry Washington, Megan Thee Stallion, and Jessie Greene.

ABOUT THE AUTHOR

Law Roach is a stylist and image architect who has worked with A-list celebrities including Zendaya, Céline Dion, Anne Hathaway, Kerry Washington, Anya Taylor-Joy, Venus Williams, Lewis Hamilton, Tom Holland, and many more. He is the first African American to be featured on the cover of the *Hollywood Reporter*'s Most Powerful Stylists issue. He is the co-host of E!'s eccentric new fashion competition series *OMG Fashun* and is a judge on hit TV shows such as *RuPaul's Drag Race*. Roach has been interviewed and featured at length in outlets including the *New York Times*, *Vogue*, *Vanity Fair*, *Harper's Bazaar*, the *Guardian*, and more. In April 2022, he was named the West Coast contributing editor of British *Vogue*.